BEYOND THE MYTHIC WEST

BEYOND THE MYTHIC WEST

STEWART L. UDALL
PATRICIA NELSON LIMERICK
CHARLES F. WILKINSON
JOHN M. VOLKMAN
WILLIAM KITTREDGE

GIBBS·SMITH PUBLISHER

PEREGRINE SMITH BOOKS
SALT LAKE CITY

In association with the Western Governors' Association

First edition
93 92 91   5 4 3 2 1

This is a Peregrine Smith Book,
published by
Gibbs Smith, Publisher
P.O. Box 667
Layton, Utah 84041

Design by J. Scott Knudsen,
Park City, Utah
Printed and bound in Hong Kong
by Everbest

**Library of Congress Cataloging-
in-Publication Data**
Beyond the mythic west / Stewart
L. Udall . . . [et al.] ; foreword by
George A. Sinner
        p.   cm.
    ISBN 0-87905-357-7
    1. West (U.S.)—Civilization—
20th century. 2. West (U.S.)—
Description and travel—1981-
3. Regionalism—West (U.S.)
4. Conservation of natural
resources—West (U.S.) I. Udall,
Stewart L. II. Western Governors'
Association.
F595.3.B48   1990
987′.033—dc20   90-7192
                          CIP

The paper used in this publication
meets the minimum requirements
of American National Standard for
Information Sciences—Perma-
nence of Paper for Printed Library
Materials, ANSI Z39.48-1984 ∞

CONTENTS

v

PUBLISHER'S NOTE

To the rest of the country and even the world, the American West has long symbolized limitless expectations and vast space, both physical and psychological.

One of our most enduring myths is that of the pioneer—rugged, independent, in search of new beginnings and conquests. Beyond that myth is the reality that the West is a fragile region that cannot accommodate the rampaging exploitation of the past. The pioneering spirit still lives on, however, in the frontier of the imagination.

Today, a new generation of westerners is shedding the sentimental and nostalgic notions of the past in favor of a new West, characterized by artistic maturity, cultural diversity, and economic sustainability. The myth of the rugged individualist is being tempered by the reality of cooperation. Along with the new myths, stories and visual images being created today, this new spirit also manifests itself by innovative economies based on high technology, small businesses, and national and international tourism.

The West is seen today as a leader on many fronts, looking only to itself for validation and existing on its own self-perpetuating energy. Long a region of borrowed culture, it is now a source of creativity in its own right, evidenced by the authors and photographers in this book.

We join with the Western Governors' Association in applauding and encouraging this new spirit.

FOREWORD

Governor George Sinner
Bismarck, North Dakota

This book, the first ever prepared by the Western Governors' Association, is first and foremost an expression of love for the West—love for the beautiful landscapes of the West, love for the resourceful people who are the foundation of the communities of the West, and love for the rich history and culture we have created in the West. We share both a sense of pride and an awareness of the challenges we face to husband our heritage and move forward on the correct course.

When we ask people the first thing that comes to mind when they hear the phrase "The American West," most will say cowboys and Indians. The genesis of this book, then, is partly founded in the desire to define the true West, the West beyond the narrow myth, the West of marvelous peoples and rich cultures, the West that is looking forward to the future.

Over the last two years, six western states celebrated their centennial anniversaries of statehood. During the anniversary celebrations many of us saw more clearly than ever the wonderful uniqueness of the West.

Stretching from the Great Plains to the Pacific Islands and from the Arctic to the Tropics, westerners every day have reminders of the many faces of nature—spectacular coastlines, mighty rivers, breathtakingly rugged mountains and badlands, stately forests, vast deserts, and incomparable resources. We also see the other face of nature at times—floods, droughts, volcanic eruptions, and earthquakes—but the sometimes harsh natural environment has raised tough-minded, strong people.

The West is indeed a rich region. Possessing a storehouse of agricultural products, timber, oil, natural gas, and precious metals, the region is well situated to ensure that, wisely and sensitively developed, our productive capacity and our food and energy stocks will be sufficient to meet future demands, even in the face of falling global reserves. In addition, the West is one of the most ethnically diverse regions of the country. Our multi-cultural heritage offers a wealth of art and a diversity of talents.

Three characteristics uniquely unite this region. Aridity has encouraged an oasis society in the inland West—growth based on water development with vast space in between. Public lands mean that control of half of the land in the West rests with federal agencies in Washington, D.C., not the state or local governments who reside here. And finally, the distances that separate here from there, offshore or on the mainland, provide the long view, a sense of isolation, enforced self-reliance, and willingness to go the extra mile.

Although the West is known for its individualists—scouts, trappers, miners, farmers, and cattlemen—most of the West's history is one of cooperation. Indian tribes, wagon trains, sailors, and Hawaiian traders who provisioned both California gold camps and whalers headed to sea, gave way to large construction crews building railroads, dams, ports and highways and to instant cities that sprang up around mineral discoveries. Westerners today are rediscovering cooperation as the "myth" for our times.

Westerners have also learned the need for diligent oversight. Few areas of the country have faced the exploiters the West has—hunters and trappers who almost exterminated the beaver and buffalo, miners who left their hazardous and unsightly tailing piles, the military who have taken over vast areas to plant missiles and to test weapons, and those who see the West's wide-open spaces as the perfect place for waste disposal. The West today is confronting the undesirable aspects of its legacy and building on its strengths. This book is a witness to maturity, a witness to continued use of resource but with the staking of a new claim— to protect environment, to work together in common respect, to celebrate the strengths of people and land—through art, enlightened public policy, and action.

Each of the authors helps define the real West, not the mythical West, and makes important suggestions for building on our remarkable set of assets. Each has deep roots in the region and understands both the complex intermingling of powerful forces in the West and the unique, somewhat insular characteristics of the West which require thoughtful solutions. Each has a powerful vision of how we can shape our future by holding onto and building from our heritage and by creating and sustaining livable communities and sensible, strong economies.

The authors reflect on one of the region's most important characteristics—making it up as we go along. Western water law copied the law of mining claims to let miners and farmers take scarce water from where it was to where it was needed. Miners, once they discovered gold or silver, were immediately hard pressed to find ways to build housing, lay out streets, get mail, provide water, and attract railroads, entertainment, businesses, newspapers, courts, school teachers, and ministers, among others. Westerners have not only made it up, we have made it work. Ideas posed in these essays fall clearly in the create-our-own-solutions tradition. We have also demonstrated a willingness to change, an increasingly valuable trait in our complex times.

One of the challenges addressed indirectly in this book is that of the many interests who see the West as "theirs." Obviously, those who have been here a long time feel that way. But so, too, do those who want to come, those who want to do business here, the many layers of government with conflicting and overlapping jurisdiction, and the established interest groups, each of which claim, often from afar, some kind of absentee stewardship. And, for that matter, the rest of the country who either wants to vacation here or wants its say because it feels it "owns" the public lands. The West does not need, nor can it tolerate, single-purpose advocates or "true believers." What we hope to accomplish through thoughtful stewardship is too important and too complex for that.

In today's world, the West needs to maintain its tradition of adaptive people and adaptive systems. The best decisions with the best chances of long-term success will come from negotiations and consensus supported by all the major parties. This book demonstrates that the West's history is one of eclectic pragmatism—people finding, borrowing, or making what was needed to survive in an orderly way. Wallace Stegner separates the West's history into exploiters and "stickers"—stickers as those who came for "the good life, not the fat life" and who "will teach the rest what life is about." This book is dedicated to the stickers, those who want to make the West work. God love them.

ACKNOWLEDGMENTS

This book would not have been possible without the leadership of the western governors, who, in supporting this effort, took a step outside their usual roles as chief executives and policymakers. We also wish to thank the many other people who contributed their wisdom and ideas toward the conception of this book, as well as those who helped bring it to fruition.

PAUSING AT THE PASS:
REFLECTIONS OF A NATIVE SON
Stewart L. Udall

T*he land was ours, before we were the land's . . . "*
Robert Frost, *The Gift Outright*

This book is a collection of essays, commissioned by the Western Governors' Association, examining the many faces of the West. In broad brush and fine detail, the authors portray the old West, the new West, the rural West, the urban-oasis West, the wilderness West, the coastal West, the mythic West, and other Wests too numerous to name.

Together, the essays represent a literary manifestation of certain venerable regional customs. Customs like putting an ear to the ground, sniffing the air, witching a well, reading spoor, and squinting at the horizon. With spyglass, divining rod, and field guide, our authors attempt to plumb the past, discern the future, and assay this evanescence we call the present. The focus of our geomancy is a five-hundred-year swath of time, extending roughly from Coronado to the year 2100. We'd like to reach forward another century, but predicting the future is like hunting into the sun: realistically, you're not likely to have much luck.

The year 1990 strikes me as an excellent vantage point. Powerful forces that have molded the West this century, most notably the Industrial Revolution and Cold War, are waning. It has been ninety-seven years since historian Frederick Jackson Turner declared the frontier closed: long enough for the West to have outgrown its callowness, short enough that we can still remember that frisky youth. The landmark-year 2000 rises like a butte on a nearby horizon, almost close enough to touch. The economy is stable, or as stable as it ever is, and in contrast with the frothy 1960s, '70s, and '80s, the social and political waters are relatively

Castle Rock, Kansas. Photo © Tom Till.

1

serene. If experience is any guide, however, this hiatus won't last: soon, no doubt, the winds of change will be keening in our ears.

On a personal note, I turned seventy this year. Three-score-and-ten is a high divide, and I'm not sure how much higher I'm going. For me, then, this seems like a good time to pause at the pass, to find a comfortable seat out of the breeze, a place to tally up the memories, dreams, and, above all, hopes of a native son.

I'm a *viejo* now, an old man, and my life meanders back over this century like a road in a Georgia O'Keeffe painting. I don't dwell on the past, but I think any intelligent appraisal of the future must start there. As the West contemplates the advent of the twenty-first century, it is vital for its citizens and political leaders to understand its advantages and glories, as well as the historical causes of its successes and failures. If I were to chronicle the history that I have witnessed as the ancient Anasazi Indians did, by pecking petroglyphs with a stone hammer into a sandstone cliff, what images would I depict?

I would start with three animals. Sheep. Cow. Grizzly bear. Growing up in northeastern Arizona in the Mormon hamlet of St. Johns during the 1920s, I herded the first two and listened raptly to stories of the third. Although the West had been "settled" for decades, it was still in many ways a remote frontier where telephones, electricity, and pavement were rare. Indeed, much of Arizona remained as wild as ever, and to a young boy the ponderosa-pine-clad mountains beyond our green fields beckoned with ineffable promise. A few trips up there, to cut fence posts and fish for trout, hooked me on wilderness—the grizzly's stronghold—for life.

My grandfather had arrived in St. Johns in the 1880s. Leaving Kanab, Utah, he led fifty families on a two-hundred-mile-trek across a stretch of barren desert where, even today, few people live. By the time I was born, the saints had been scrabbling out a living on the banks of the Little Colorado for forty years. Hard working, determined, fortified with righteousness, they had made an imprint on the land—but not much of one.

Our cattle and sheep, and those being grazed in other western states, were another matter. Back then, before the Dust Bowl and Great Depression hit like bills come due, there was little appreciation for how, and how fast, the ax, the cow, the plow, and barbed wire were reshaping the West. In 1900, when Teddy Roosevelt became president, there were an estimated thirty million sheep and fifteen million cattle on the open range, or twice as many domestic ungulates as there previously had been wild ones. Overgrazing and clearcutting of forests on federal land were rampant. Although Roosevelt was born in New York City, the two years he spent as a cattleman in North Dakota inspired him to take on the ''empire builders'' who were plundering the West. Espousing the newly minted tenets of resource conservation, Roosevelt signed bills establishing millions of acres of new national forests, national wildlife refuges, and national parks, including Crater Lake, Mesa Verde, and Grand Canyon.

Back to the petroglyph cliff. This time to diagram that prototypical twentieth-century western scene: a canyon, a river, and a gigantic dam swarming with hordes of ant-sized construction workers. As a Mormon, I was born with a shovel in my hand, irrigation my birthright. (As we worked in the fields, guiding water here and there, my father was wont to say, ''Son, irrigation is a *science.*'') But the dam I depict is not one of our puny earthen jobs that was sluiced away by the next flash flood. No, this is a permanent structure, engineered for the ages, millions of cubic yards of white concrete plugging a black gorge—Hoover Dam.

The Reclamation Era, begun by Teddy Roosevelt in 1902, matured in the thirties under his cousin FDR. During the bleak days of the depression, it was a heartening sign of regional panache that two of the three great engineering wonders that moved forward on schedule—the Empire State Building, Hoover Dam, and the Golden Gate Bridge—were located in the West. Work at Hoover went on twenty-four hours a day, and I can vividly recall the giant floodlights and huge cranes I saw during a nighttime visit to the construction site as a teenager.

Forty of the fifty highest dams in the United States are in the West. The seventeen highest are all western dams, and, with one exception, they were built in a thirty-five-year period between the time I turned seventeen and fifty-two. We harnessed the Missouri, Colorado, Sacramento, and Columbia Rivers as our fathers had done oxen, converted

There is little appreciation for how, and how fast, the ax, the cow, the plow, and barbed wire were reshaping the West.

3

their power to electricity, and diverted their water to fields and cities. Hoover and Grand Coulee were celebrated on the flickering newsreels. And why not?—this was plumbing on a Promethean scale. With gigantic dams and tens of thousands of miles of canals, we had, as the newscasters said, exchanged the dusty bonds of aridity for the lush fields of the future.

For anyone of my generation, the next image is a stark given. Many planes dropping many bombs on many ships—Pearl Harbor. No event has ever had a more profound impact on the West than did World War II. After Pearl Harbor, vast tracts of government-owned land in the West were consecrated to military purposes. Favorable flying conditions encouraged the air force to locate the bulk of its airfields here; the army found inexpensive sites for the big training bases it needed; and the war in the Pacific impelled the navy to build huge installations all along the coast from San Diego to Anchorage.

I spent the war flying over Italy, gunner in a B-24. The plane had probably been fabricated in Seattle, the copper in it mined in Arizona or Montana. When I returned home after three years, I was thankful to see that my beloved West had been spared the devastation visited on Europe and Asia; on the contrary, the region had prospered, its storehouse of oil, natural resources, hydropower, and minerals being essential to winning the war. Although the bombing of Hiroshima and Nagasaki had ended one war, it was soon to be followed by another, the Cold War, in which the West would be, in a sense, at ground zero.

Although millions of soldiers were demobilized in the years after World War II, neither the West nor the nation returned to pre-war patterns of economics. The Soviet Union's surprising speed in developing atomic weapons and the Korean War combined to keep U.S. military spending at a high level. The crash effort to develop nuclear weapons that began in the 1950s gave a westward tilt to defense expenditures and spawned a new image of the West—a mushroom cloud rising over the Nevada desert, heralding the Atomic Age.

For five decades the West has unselfishly borne the heaviest burden in the production of America's atomic weapons. No state was left untouched by the nuclear embrace. Uranium was mined in Utah, Arizona, New Mexico, Colorado, and Wyoming, and refined in Washington and Idaho. The bombs were built in California and New Mexico, and then tested in Nevada. Intercontinental missiles were planted in silos in Montana, Wyoming, and the Dakotas like some lethal root crop waiting to be harvested. Nuclear-armed submarines were stationed off Hawaii, Alaska, and the West Coast.

The economic impacts of trillions of federal defense dollars have been significant—boom towns, jobs, and prosperity. In recent years, however, as radioactive wastes piled up and civilians began dying of cancer, it has become increasingly clear that the West has paid a heavy price. Ahead looms the long, difficult, and expensive cleanup. New Mexico and Nevada bear a special burden in this regard, having been chosen to "host" the nation's nuclear waste repositories.

In 1960, President John F. Kennedy appointed me Secretary of Interior. Vietnam and civil rights were in the air. But there was another item on the national agenda—the environment—and now I must return to the cliff to etch in the shoulders of the Grand Canyon, where the dam builders would be, for the first time, stopped. From the days of John Muir, the West has always been the chief locus of the American conservation movement, and the heated controversy over two proposed dams in the Grand Canyon inspired many citizens to reconsider the price of Progress. Reclamation, we learned, had costs as well as benefits.

The sixties were an exciting time in Washington. In 1962 Rachel Carson sounded the alarm about the unrestricted use of pesticides in *Silent Spring.* Motivated by health concerns and a desire to protect their natural heritage, tens of thousands of Americans joined conservation groups. Environmentalists flexed their new-found muscle to pass the Wilderness Act in 1964, the Endangered Species Act in 1966. In 1968 the National Wild and Scenic Rivers Act was approved, and in 1969 the National Environmental Protection Act brought the "environmental impact statement" into our jargon. In that same year, *Apollo 11* landed on the moon. There Neil Armstrong found an inhospitable world whose barren harshness only accentuated the life-giving loveliness of Spaceship Earth.

Of all the images from which I might select to depict the 1970s, I'll choose two: a Saudi sheik and an oil pipeline snaking across the tundra.

In 1973 the United States woke up in an OPEC stranglehold. Americans were outraged and frightened. Why had this happened? The answer was simple, so simple it was easily overlooked. In that year, to power our industry, businesses, cars, and homes, Americans used per capita as much energy as that contained in 60 barrels, or 2,500 gallons of gasoline. This is the equivalent of lighting 650 kitchen matches every *minute* for an entire year.

Two hundred and ten million people living the most energy-intensive lifestyle ever seen on the planet, our response to OPEC's blackmail was part panic, part disbelief. Terrified that our economy was about to seize for lack of vital fluids, the government embarked on a massive quest for more energy—without first asking whether it wouldn't make more sense and be far cheaper to use energy more efficiently.

The West has always been America's natural resources pantry, and the late '70s and early '80s were boom times as the federal government, multinational energy companies, and utilities spent billions drilling oil wells, building the Alaska pipeline, constructing nuclear power plants, and tinkering with exotic technologies like synfuels and coal gasification. But then, as energy prices rose, Americans began buying gas-sipping cars, insulating attics, caulking windows. As consumers opted to save money by saving energy, shortages were transformed into gluts, and many of the megaprojects succumbed to a fatal attack of market forces.

The bust was sharp and painful, devastating to the oil patch and its workers. It took some years to understand that it had been a blessing in disguise, that the Northwest did not need five new nuclear power plants; that our air would have been fouled if every coal plant on the drawing boards had been built; and that scenic western Colorado would have been devastated by an oil shale industry of the size envisaged.

I spent the 1980s in Phoenix, practicing law and observing, with increasing disbelief, the sunbelt's growth. Stone in hand, standing at the foot of the cliff, I'm stumped: How does one portray the sudden blossoming of western cities that took place this century? Los Angeles, up seventyfold since 1900. Honolulu twentyfold over the same period. Aptly-named named Phoenix two hundredfold, from 5,000 in 1900 to almost a million today. I have lived with this runaway locomotive all my life, but only recently did I ask: Where is it headed? And think, Ho! Four million people in Phoenix by 2050?! Is this prediction, fate, fantasy, lunacy—or all of the above?

This growth has occurred with such rapidity that I must force myself to remember that when my grandfather founded St. Johns in the 1880s, the largest city west of St. Louis was Butte, Montana—and that, for a short season, the gold-mining boomtown of Tombstone, Arizona, had more inhabitants than San Francisco. Few parts of the world have ever experienced such explosive growth. "Two lifetimes ago, the West was home to about 250,000 people," says geographer Dennis Brownridge. "Now it has 50 million—an increase of 20,000 percent. If the rest of the world had grown at the same rate, we'd be staggering under the weight of 200 billion people."

That is a dizzying thought, and so for my peace of mind, let me cease reminiscing and climb down from this airy perch. Let's turn for a moment to the present. On what verities can everybody agree, what is the western bedrock of today?

As we have noted, the West as a whole is more populated and richer than ever. (California alone has more people and a larger economy than Canada.) As the region's economy has diversified, the relative importance of ranching, farming, logging, and mining has declined. In recent years, as the East lost manufacturing jobs, the West gained them. The traditional resource-based economy is not, however, as some have claimed, dying. Although the oil exploration business is slumbering, 20 percent of America's domestic oil rises from the Alaska's North Slope. In Nevada, Idaho, Colorado, and South Dakota gold mines are booming. Agriculture, ranching, logging, and fishing remain economic bulwarks. Huge reserves of western coal and natural gas have yet to be tapped.

In addition to manufacturing of all kinds, another industry that has grown remarkably over the past three decades is tourism based on sightseeing and outdoor recreation such as fishing, hunting, skiing, surfing, backpacking, boating, and white-water rafting. This no-bust business is based on the West's long suit—the charisma of its clean, spacious landscapes. There's an old cliche that "you can't eat the scenery," but today more and more tourists, including eighteen million foreigners in 1987,

I have lived with this runaway locomotive all my life, but only recently did I ask: Where is it headed?

7

are happily paying for the privilege of feasting their eyes on our back-yard. A typical reaction, from a Swiss visitor: "You are very lucky to live here. We are so crowded we dream of open space."

Although large areas of that open space remain pristine, it's also true that you don't have to look hard to find places where humanity has unraveled the region's wonder. Still, even if the natural tapestry of the West has been frayed, our landscape has retained much of its unique appeal. All in all, I think many people will agree that, whether you choose Fairbanks, Portland, Provo, Prescott, Pueblo, Las Cruces, Laramie, Honolulu, or some other western city or town, there's no better place to live.

As a place to rear children and enjoy a healthy lifestyle, a case can be made that the West is now the most attractive region in the country; simply put, it is the "last best place." This is not boosterism but fact, supported by irrefutable evidence. Today, as in Horace Greeley's time, people vote with their feet; that the West is now the fastest-growing region of America suggests that millions of people believe their future lies here. By any standard—dynamic cities, economic vitality, ethnic diversity, environmental cleanliness, sparkling beaches, recreational opportunities or wildlife—the West has an edge.

Even in culture and education, areas where in the past it was often suggested that we suffered a provincial impoverishment, our star is shining. Most large western cities now boast symphonies, libraries, museums, and universities that can compare with those in the East.

To say that the West offers its citizens an unrivaled quality of life is to raise two other questions: Is it possible to keep it that way? And, if so, how?

These questions have spawned a recent torrent of analysis. Bill Hornby, senior editor of the *Denver Post,* believes that the "West's superior livability" is its most powerful magnet for investment. In his view, the West has a glowing future if it "nurtures its increasing numbers of people by sustaining their environment, education, and racial harmony."

Tom Peters, America's maverick management consultant, is bullish, too. The West, he says, is a place where people from all over the world want to live and invest. According to Peters, the information revolution and Pacific Century have arrived—good news particularly for California, Oregon, Washington, Hawaii, and Alaska.

Although I, too, am optimistic, before we set forth across that century I think it behooves us to contemplate five challenges rising like thunderstorms on the horizon. In my view, the West's problems and its potential are inextricably intertwined: solving the former will help us realize the latter.

CHALLENGES FOR THE WEST

One peril some gloomy observers have prophesied is the eventual "depopulation" of the rural Rockies and northern Plains. In 1989 Washington, Idaho, Montana, Wyoming, and North and South Dakota celebrated their hundredth birthdays. *Newsweek* marked the occasion with a doom-and-gloom eulogy subtitled "Amid scarcity and broken dreams, six western states mark 100 hard years at the end of the cracked whip." The article—and others like it—argued that the "frontier's precious vein of promise and possibility is running out." It quoted a rancher as saying that Wyoming's future may be "wolves, Wal-Marts, and waste"—garbage trucked in from distant states to be buried in empty coal mines. This, I think, is largely rubbish.

Although the last decade has been hard on the rural West, with rolling recessions affecting every sector of the economy and the population in some areas falling, a compelling case can be made that the region is on the verge of a renaissance. Before making it, however, I think one must first shuck the boomer mentality that more people are necessarily better, in favor of the ecological precept of *carrying capacity*. If Wyoming can now support only as many people as it does antelope (about 475,000 of each currently), is that necessarily a bad thing? Should the fact that as many people ride the subway in New York City each day as live in the Dakotas be a cause for grave concern? Should we pity those counties in Colorado that have larger populations of elk than people? I can understand Montana's concern about losing a congressional seat after the next census. But even if this comes to pass, the state will still have two senators, one congressman, a spirited stable of novelists, and some of the finest trout fishing outside Alaska.

9

In truth, parts of the West may always be an outback, lightly populated by a rugged and resourceful citizenry. Again, this is a strength—and will only become more so if human population soars, as predicted, from five billion today to ten or fourteen billion by 2100. Space, solitude, blue skies, wild animals roaming free—these will be precious assets in the decades ahead. Indeed, if current trends continue, Africa will have lost its wildlife by 2100, leaving Alaska, Canada, and the mountain West to serve as the world's last "Serengeti."

As for the rural West's economic prospects, the dawning of the post-industrial economy, demographic trends, and a rebound in commodity prices all suggest that a brighter future lies ahead. In this FedEx age of computers, fax machines, modems, and overnight mail, any town anywhere can participate in the international economy. These new telecommunications technologies have made many jobs and businesses portable. Instead of being forced to live where the work is, people can now work where *they want to live.* This revolutionary development will have a profound impact on our region.

The migration of people, businesses, and retirees fleeing the crowded and expensive coasts is already beginning to buttress rural economies. For example, the outdoor clothing manufacturer Patagonia recently moved its mail order operation from Ventura, California, to Bozeman, Montana, instantly becoming one of that community's largest employers. Although this trend seems sure to grow, for the short term the northern Plains will continue to be reliant on ranching, farming, mining, and tourism. But the outlook for these occupations is not as bleak as *Newsweek* suggests. Global grain supplies are now at their lowest level in decades; in a food-short world, demand for western grain and beef can only rise. The mining industry, which some commentators had all but buried in the mid-1980s, is today leaner and more productive than ever; environmental regulations are boosting demand for low-sulfur western coal; and concerns about global warming have made clean-burning natural gas the best fuel for the '90s. Tourism, according to some studies, may be the world's largest industry by the year 2000.

Decades ago, busted towns often had no choice but to wither and die. Today, however, communities that suffer economic reversals aren't necessarily condemned to a tumbleweed's fate. Indeed, with resilience and diversification as the watchwords, every town or region can initiate programs that will invigorate its economy and make it a more attractive place to live and visit. For evidence of this, all we need to do is look around. The first thing we see is that gateway towns (Jackson, Wyoming; Moab, Utah; Whitefish, Montana; Flagstaff, Arizona; Fairbanks, Alaska; Cody, Wyoming; Rapid City, South Dakota) near national parks and other tourist attractions are thriving. By exploiting assets such as location, climate, or scenery, many communities deeper in the hinterlands have also wrought a similar alchemy. When Exxon abandoned the oil shale business, Parachute, Colorado, became a ghost town overnight. Today Parachute is a thriving community of retirees. Hood River, Oregon, has become a mecca for windsurfers. Pueblo, Colorado, once a steel town dependent on the local mill, has revitalized its economy by aggressively recruiting new companies with free land. Many old mining towns—including Butte, Montana; Bisbee, Arizona; Park City, Utah; and Telluride, Colorado—have been resuscitated by light industry, tourism, skiing, or, in Butte's case, newly reopened mines. These towns weren't saved by corporate "white knights"; they bootstrapped themselves back into the black using a blend of local capital, expertise, civic cooperation, and ingenuity.

If it is true that wages in rural areas are unlikely ever to match those in big cities, neither will the cost of housing. Few rural towns boast many high-paying jobs, but their proximity to clear air, good hunting, skiing, and fishing represents, for families looking to raise their children in a wholesome setting, a "second paycheck." My own experience growing up in a rural area tells me this country needs small towns and modest-sized cities. We need them as slow-lane refuges where people overwhelmed by urban stress can find peace and quietude. We need them as a reminder of the lifestyles and values of an older, perhaps saner, America. And we need them because people in small towns and cities often are more attuned to the natural world, less blindly materialistic, at once more community centered and self-reliant. Was it an accident that tiny hamlets on the Canadian border produced such wise and perceptive luminaries as Wallace Stegner, Eric Sevareid, and Chet Huntley?

Decades ago, busted towns often had no choice but to wither and die. Today, however, communities that suffer economic reversals aren't necessarily condemned to a tumbleweed's fate.

As a threat to the West's continued prosperity, depopulation pales in comparison to the energy problem. The inability of the United States to develop a sensible energy policy is now in its seventeenth year, an astounding failure whose costs we must, I fear, sooner or later pay. Gasoline is now cheaper in real terms than at any time since the Korean War—but this cannot last. Petroleum is a nonrenewable resource, yet we price it at half the cost of milk, a renewable one which cows will still be providing long after the oil is gone. The idling auto and gas guzzler have reappeared on our streets. Every twenty minutes Americans use as much oil as the Exxon *Valdez* spilled. If imports were cut off, our proven domestic reserves would last for just five years at current rates of consumption. Granted, there's more oil to be found, but not, in anybody's view, a whole lot more.

Our growing dependence on imported oil is eroding the financial health of America. The $49 billion we spent last year on foreign petroleum represents almost half our trade deficit. As the nation becomes more and more dependent on oil from abroad, our ability to control our own economic destiny diminishes. Yes, another oil crisis would be a boon for our domestic oil industry, but its long-term impacts would be negative. Far better to extract our petroleum at a steady rate than for the oil industry to pump itself out of business in one frenzied paroxysm. Moreover, as the *Valdez* accident illustrates, the environmental costs of searching for and transporting oil fall disproportionately on the West. Many remaining prospects—offshore California, the Overthrust Belt in the Rockies, and the Arctic National Wildlife Refuge—lie in pristine areas which we should preserve as a storehouse for future generations.

What do we do when the gasoline runs out? Can the farm states fill part of the energy gap with ethanol? Can the oil states fill another part with methanol and natural gas? While waiting for the federal government to devise a coherent energy strategy, what *should* the West do?

Four things come to mind. First, with tax incentives and legislation, states can encourage auto companies to produce, and consumers to buy, more fuel-efficient cars. Second, our cities must begin investing in mass transportation. Third, states can adopt least-cost planning regulations for utilities and stiffer insulation requirements for buildings. (The nation loses as much energy through our windows as flows through the Alaska pipeline.) Fourth, the sunbelt should establish a goal of leading the nation towards a new future based on renewable energy and solar power. To date, however, we've just begun. (Cloudy Tokyo has more solar hot water heaters than does the entire U.S.—a sobering statistic.)

Some progress is being made. Hawaii gets nearly 20 percent of its energy from renewable sources. Engineers at Boeing have recently developed a 37-percent-efficient photovoltaic cell. Scientists at Los Alamos National Laboratory and the Solar Energy Research Institute are also in hot pursuit of photovoltaic cells that could produce electricity as cheaply as coal. In California, Luz International is the world leader in solar power plants. The sun-blessed West should build on these initiatives. Could there be a better place for solar-electric cars than Phoenix or L.A.?

The next major problem/opportunity the West, or at least most of it, faces is an old one—water. In arid lands, water, too, is a form of energy. Westerners often say that water is precious, but in reality our "lifeblood" is used inefficiently and even wantonly wasted throughout our region, a situation that we can no longer afford.

The benefits of better water management are manifest. Water efficiency can forestall or eliminate the need to drown valuable rivers with expensive dams. Consumers benefit through reduced water and sewer fees and again through smaller water-heating bills. Farmers can reduce energy bills and harmful salt levels in their fields by not over-irrigating. Leaving more water in-stream is good for salmon, trout, fishermen, ducks, geese, deer, hunters, kayakers, and rafters. There is every reason to use water efficiently. Everybody wins, nobody loses.

In recent years, some water-short cities, including Tucson, Santa Monica, and Morro Bay, have discovered that the cheapest and fastest way to augment supplies is to encourage residents to shrink their lawns and install water-efficient plumbing fixtures. Since a gallon of water saved is the same as a gallon of water supplied, xeriscaping, faucet aerators, and low-flow toilets can be thought of as small dams. The EPA probably did Denver residents a favor by recently denying the city permission to build a new $1-billion dam. In response, the Denver Water Board launched an efficiency campaign that has the potential to save as much water as

13

the dam would have produced, at one-sixth the cost.

Eighty percent of the West's water is used on farms and ranches. Even small gains in agricultural efficiency could produce a bountiful crop of "new" water that farmers could sell to thirsty cities. To help reap this harvest, gypsum blocks and electronic sensors can be used to monitor soil moisture levels. Leaky canals can be lined with concrete. Arizona cotton farmers have demonstrated that underground pipes can put water and fertilizers where they are needed—in the root zone—while boosting profits and saving half the water required for conventional irrigation. Unfortunately, in some states "use it or lose it" regulations discourage farmers and ranchers from capturing potential savings. Such laws should be repealed and replaced with conservation incentives.

As John Volkman describes in his essay, integrated watershed management is another tool for revamping obsolescent water practices. In theory, there's no reason why ranchers, industry, Indian tribes, environmentalists, and federal and state agencies along the Missouri, Platte, Rio Grande, and Colorado Rivers couldn't establish regional planning entities similar to the one now operating in the Columbia watershed. Clearly, it makes more sense to mediate disputes over water rights, endangered species, recreational impacts, and hydropower development in a roundtable setting than before a judge.

There is also vast room for improvement in the management of the West's groundwater. The pollution of aquifers with carcinogens, radioactive wastes, and pesticides is a widespread affliction with no apparent cure. In many areas, (the Ogallala Aquifer that underlies eleven million acres of the Plains is the classic example) farmers are rapidly depleting "fossil" groundwater that has slowly accumulated over millions of years. Groundwater withdrawals presently exceed natural recharge by some twenty billion gallons *per day* in the West. As water tables fall, pumping costs soar. Eventually, farmland must be abandoned or converted to dryland crops. Recognizing the need to reform existing practices, many western governors are now advocating new water marketing and conservation arrangements that will encourage wiser use of our most precious resource.

The fourth great challenge our region faces is coping with the coming new era in East-West relations. The Cold War is over and the United States now must retool its defense industry to convert military production to peaceful ends. This will have a staggering impact on many western states. (In California, for example, the federal government last year spent $90 billion on defense.) Individual plants and workers may be hard hit as defense spending winds down. New Mexico Senator Pete Domenici predicts that military contracts awarded to his state will be cut by 40–60 percent over the next ten years, and the story may be similar elsewhere. But the West's defense industry is destined to shrink, not vanish. For the foreseeable future, America will continue to need a strong military and nuclear deterrent. What's more, we still face the immense task of cleaning up our nuclear weapons facilities, a job the Department of Energy estimates will cost $80–180 billion. The majority of these monies will be spent in the West and will thus partially offset the defense cuts. Although the guns-to-butter transformation will be wrenching, the productive investment of multibillions now dedicated to defense should, in time, create a healthier, more vibrant economy.

The fifth and final great challenge the West faces is protecting its urban, rural, and natural environments, an overarching theme that touches on all our aspirations. As Charles Wilkinson explains in his essay, if we can protect our wilderness areas, rangelands, national parks, air, and water, the West will prosper. If we don't, it won't, for the simple reason that in much of the West the environment now *is* the economy.

But we must not forget that "environment" has social connotations, too. Seven of every ten westerners live in cities; for them, the most important environment is the urban one. The problems of the homeless and poor afflict large cities in our region as they do in the East. Can we make our cities more livable? Reduce the drugs, congestion, poverty, and crime that sometimes gives urban living a nightmarish pall? Narrow the alarming gulf between haves and have-nots?

Beginning with LBJ's War on Poverty, America has, in fits and starts, labored to improve urban life. Our record is spotty, but our successes and failures have given us a good idea of what works. Education, particularly in early childhood, works. Helping young people attain a sense of self-worth works. Providing job training works, particularly when it's

We must not forget that "environment" has social connotations, too. Seven of every ten westerners live in cities; for them, the most important environment is the urban one.

combined with programs that help men and women climb out of the underclass. In recent years, though, the bottom rungs on that ladder have been sawed off as federal funds for job programs have been slashed. Surely in the coming decade the federal government will invest some of the peace dividend in our cities.

Another thing states can do to enhance their social environment is to help Indian tribes develop their human and natural resources. In the past, some state leaders have disparaged Indian reservations as federal enclaves best ignored. Unfortunately, this shortsighted approach has hampered the ability of Native Americans to make positive contributions to the general welfare.

Here, too, there are positive examples that could be widely emulated. In New Mexico, the Pueblo Indians have successfully preserved the artistic lineaments of their culture; they are now an integral part of the tourism dynamo that helps drive that state's economy. A new Indian-owned hotel under construction in Santa Fe demonstrates how tribal development can attract investment capital that will benefit all New Mexicans. In neighboring Arizona, the White Mountain Apaches own many valuable parcels of undeveloped land, are stewards of some of that state's best-managed forests, and operate its finest ski resort. In Alaska, some Inuit and Indian tribes have skillfully managed their natural resources.

After a century of benign neglect and sometimes outright hostility, the time is ripe to begin forging new bonds of cooperation between Indians and state governments. In 1989, the western governors collectively affirmed tribal sovereignty and pledged to a policy of joint resolution of conflicts.

Out on the land, we also have some healing to do. The West is pocked with scars and suppurating sores: uranium tailings, toxic and chemical wastes, overgrazed riparian areas, clearcuts, polluted streams, and abandoned strip mines blemish our region. During the next decades, environmental restoration, or ecology in action, must become a priority. We need a new cadre of dedicated conservationists to heal our rivers, clean our air, restore the range, revegetate strip mines, and generally right past environmental wrongs.

Our national parks remain a bright spot. Although they face a panoply of pressures, including air pollution, acid rain, and aircraft over-flights, the parks remain in relatively good shape. Each year more and more Americans come to visit, and foreigners have discovered them as well. This is all the more reason to finish the job of designating new parks, wild and scenic rivers, wildlife refuges, prairie preserves, wetlands, and wilderness areas in every western state where worthy candidates exist.

There are many valid arguments one can make for preserving land in its natural state. Former New Mexico senator Clinton Anderson articulated one of the best: "Wilderness is an anchor to windward. Knowing it is there, we can also know that we are still a rich nation, tending to our resources as we should—not a people in despair searching every last nook and cranny of our land for a board of lumber, a barrel of oil, a blade of grass, or a tank of water."

Wilderness areas provide our purest water and meet a host of other human needs—recreation, quiet, natural beauty, spiritual inspiration. But preservation of our natural resources isn't merely good environmental policy; it's also good economic policy. Spacious, unspoiled landscapes pay hidden economic dividends that will only grow more valuable in an increasingly crowded world.

STRATEGIES FOR THE FUTURE

From this vantage, the twenty-first century is a mirage shimmering on the horizon. It is what the Spanish explorers called a *despoblado,* an unpopulated wilderness. No one alive today will live to see our western civilization reach the other side. Contemplating that journey, it is immensely difficult to predict what tools and provisions and strategies we should carry so that our children's children can arrive safely.

But if I were quartermaster, I would emphasize, first, education. At the moment, America is neglecting its children, a symptom of our general disdain for sacrifice and foresight. This is folly of the highest order. If we in the West are serious about our future, every child must receive the best possible education. This is particularly true for disadvantaged and minority children growing up on reservations, in ghettos and impoverished rural towns. Their education should begin early with Head Start and focus on history, geography, science, art, and mathematics. Every child should learn a second language and become computer literate.

As I have noted, a second legacy we must provide the next generation is a healthy natural environment, with ample resources to sustain them. I won't belabor the point, except to say that we should encourage our kids to leave *their* kids a better environment that we have left *them*. If there's a single litmus test for the West's well-being a century from now it might be: Is the sky blue? Can you drink from the rivers and breathe the air?

As we outfit ourselves for the next century, we should also recall an old rule of thumb heeded by all savvy travelers: dump excess baggage. Lacking draft animals, some pioneers walked from Missouri to Utah pushing handcarts the whole way. A few hours of this grinding labor inspired a careful taking-stock. Do we need all of this stuff? What can we afford to jettison? Not surprisingly, the immigrant trails were littered with oak bureaus and trunks leaden with nonessential keepsakes.

But the excess baggage I'm speaking of isn't material objects; it is ideas, attitudes, laws, and institutions—outdated mental and bureaucratic constructs as awkward and burdensome as any anvil.

Take racial animosity, for example. In her perceptive essay, Patricia Limerick describes the human history of the West as resembling a rendezvous—and not just of white men and red Indians. The West has never had a homogeneous culture and today there are more tribes at the rendezvous than ever. Sioux, Chinese, Hispanics, Anglos, Blacks, Laotians, Guatemalans, Catholics, Russians, Nez Perce, Mormons . . . the list is almost endless. The West is not a melting pot, it's a rich ethnic, religious, and racial slumgullion that nourishes all of us. Here in New Mexico, ethnicity spices our food, architecture, art, politics, literature, clothing, and language. (*Colorado Plateau* is a Spanish word married to a French one.) Who wants to live in a monoculture?

But it's important to teach our children that cultural diversity is not just objects—it's *people.* I look forward to the day when more Anglos cherish their Hispanic neighbors as much as they now do Mexican food, when they value a Navajo as highly as a Navajo blanket.

18

Of the many outdated laws that burden the West, the most sclerotic is the 1872 Mining Law. The days of the solitary prospector and his burro are long gone, but the responsible development of the West's mineral resources continues to be impeded by this superannuated legislation. The 1922 Colorado River Compact, on the other hand, has not entirely outlived its usefulness, but a brisk scrubbing of its most barnacle-encrusted provisions, particularly those relating to the transfer of water between states, is in order.

The federal government manages fully half of all western land. Despite the efforts of many capable and dedicated employees, few federal agencies have kept pace with the times. The Bureau of Land Management, the U.S. Forest Service, the Bureau of Indian Affairs, and the Bureau of Reclamation now recognize that their most urgent task is to redefine their missions and reinvigorate their sometimes-tired thinking. Before leaving this topic, I should mention one agency that has done its job too well: the Animal Damage Control division of the U.S. Department of Agriculture. It's time we stopped slaughtering predators for being predators. Let's put away the traps and poison.

Of all the decrepit notions still deep-seated in the West, perhaps the most invidious is the belief that plunder equals progress. In this regard, I'm reminded of the memorable malapropism uttered by one western senator: "If we don't stop shearing the wool off the goose that lays the golden egg, we are going to pump the well dry."

The period when the West could satisfy much of the country's rapacious appetite for natural resources is drawing to a close. Most of the old-growth timber has been cut, the oil pumped, the high-grade silver and gold mined. The pantry is not empty, but it's time to begin husbanding what's left. Over the long run, certainly by the time our children's children are grown, our culture must come to grips with the inherent inconsistency of sustained growth on a finite planet. From a historical perspective, the passing of the Bonanza Era was inevitable. The notion of the West as cornucopia was a falsehood that could only be sustained as long as human numbers were small. Our natural resources can no longer support this seductive illusion. At this point, we should aim to minimize resource consumption and pollution, while maximizing well-being.

But the excess baggage I'm speaking of isn't material objects; it is ideas, attitudes, laws, and institutions . . .

19

Arizona. Photo © **Monty Roessel.**

William Ruckelshaus, former administrator of the Environmental Protection Agency, has said that developing a sustainable economy will be "a modification of society comparable in scale to the Industrial Revolution. The undertaking will be absolutely unique in humanity's stay on earth." Although life in a sustainable society may be more humane, spiritually rewarding, and peaceful than what we have today, making the transition will be slow, arduous, and demanding—all the more reason to begin sooner rather than later. Here, too, we have an inspiring model: Hopi farmers who have survived on their desert mesa, in an area of little rainfall and marginal soils, for many centuries.

When it comes time to wish our children Godspeed on their journey into the future, we will probably want to proffer some last-minute advice. There is a story, perhaps apocryphal, told about the nineteenth-century

Colorado gold and silver baron H. A. W. Tabor that is relevant. Lying on his deathbed, Tabor called his wife to his side for final instructions on the disposition of his various mines. "Hold on to the Matchless" he whispered, then died.

Hold on to the Matchless. These words have resonance even today, although not in their literal sense. Baby Doe Tabor faithfully held onto the Matchless Mine for decades after her husband's death and died penniless guarding its door, waiting for a bonanza which was never to come. For our children, I hope the lesson will be easier.

Instead of "holding on to *the Matchless*"—the old way of doing things—we should teach them to hold onto *that which is matchless*. If we old and middle-aged ones, we *viejos* and *viejas,* teach our children that the West is a special region, a matchless environment, provide them

Bell Mountain, Lemhi Range, Idaho. Photo ©️ Brent Smith.

21

Totem Pole, Monument Valley, Arizona. Photo © Martin Price.

with opportunities to explore the hidden recesses in its dazzling land-scape, encourage them to relish their racial and ethnic diversity, and allow their character to be shaped by loving families, compassionate teachers, healthy cities, clean skies, running rivers, and distant horizons, then our hopes for their safe journey may, in the fullness of time, be realized.

Having done that, our task will be complete.

Joshua Tree National Monument, California. Photo © George Wuerthner.

Middle Fork of Birch Creek, Bob Marshall Wilderness, Montana. Photo © George Wuerthner.

Wind Cave National Park, South Dakota. Photo © Tom Till.

Lamoille Canyon, Ruby Mountains, Nevada. Photo © Tom Till

Arapaho Pass, Indian Peaks Wilderness, Colorado. Photo © Martin Price

Arrigetch Peaks, Gates of Arctic National Park, Alaska. Photo © George Wuerthner.

Coyote, Nebraska plains. Photo © Jon Farrar.

The Racetrack, Death Valley National Monument, California. Photo © Tom Till.

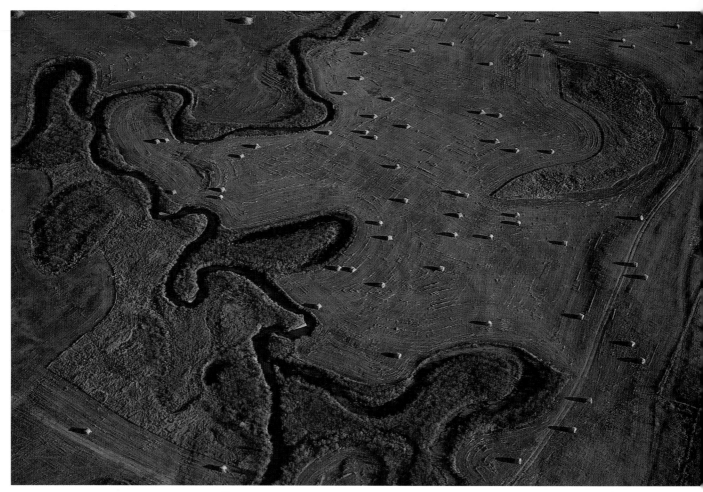

Goose Creek at Elsmere, Nebraska. Photo © Jon Farrar

Yellowstone Falls, Yellowstone National Park, Wyoming. Photo © George Wuerthner

THE RENDEZVOUS MODEL OF WESTERN HISTORY

Patricia Nelson Limerick

In my little restaurant at Monterey, we have sat down to table, day after day, a Frenchman, two Portuguese, an Italian, a Mexican, and a Scotsman: we had for common visitors an American from Illinois, a nearly pure-blood Indian woman, and a naturalised Chinese; and from time to time a Switzer and a German came down from country ranches for the night.
Robert Louis Stevenson in California, 1879–1880

The entertainment commenced with serving each with a little tobacco, then our musical instruments . . . played up a lively air. Which from many of the Natives, now hearing for the first time, caused a general exclamation of wonder and pleasure—This was followed by a request for them to dance, which they did willingly, then our seamen danced in their turn, and so the thing went alternately, in a little time the Natives entered fully into the spirit of the Amusement . . .
Captain Rochfort Maguire off Point Barrow, Alaska, 1854

On a family vacation in the 1950s, we visited the Russian outpost at Fort Ross, north of San Francisco. As a child of the Cold War, I could not get this historic site to make sense. Russians in *California*? What on earth had they been doing there?

Addled by the relics of the Russian presence in California, I was at least clear in my choice of heroes from California history, having settled on the Spanish explorer Juan Rodriguez Cabrillo. Exploring the California coast in 1542, Cabrillo found San Diego Bay but missed San Francisco Bay, then broke an arm and died mid-voyage. But I was taken with

Businessmen. Phoenix, Arizona. Photo © Kent Knudsen.

35

Cabrillo, and the proof of this lies in the fact that I gave his name to my cat.

Calling my cat Cabrillo, and growing up in Banning, a town in Southern California bordered by the Morongo Indian Reservation and peopled by a collection of whites, Hispanics, and blacks, I received my most compelling lessons in Western American history. At my high school graduation, I sat next to Aquilino Diano Antonio Eusebio "Lee" Sapaden, and when they read that name aloud, and followed it with the name Patty Nelson, I did not feel that I had the most interesting background of any person on the stage. Lee Sapaden was Filipino, but I did not really quite know what that meant, or where, if the Philippines were in Asia, Lee had gotten all those more-or-less Hispanic names.

In the 1950s and 1960s in Banning, ethnic sensitivity was not at its height. Even well-intentioned adults often seemed more nonplussed than helpful when they tried to orient us to the facts of human diversity. In sixth grade, in Baptist Sunday school, one young Banningite finally voiced a question that had privately perplexed us all: "What exactly," she asked the teacher, "is a Jew? We keep seeing that word in the Bible, but we don't know what it means." Our teacher looked unhappy, and trapped. "Well, you all know Jeff," she said, and pointed to a boy who had just moved to town. "Jeff used to be a Jew, but now he's a Baptist."

This did not deepen our understanding of either the Bible's history or Banning's history, but it certainly stayed in my memory as a peak moment in useful perplexity. Even if I did not know where all these people came from—people at once deeply familiar and deeply mysterious to me—I knew they were *here*. I knew that western America was home to Jews, Mormons, and Baptists; Indians, blacks, and Filipinos; Hispanics, Russians, and even odd birds like myself, descendant of Danish Mormons and Scottish-English-Irish hybrids.

Firsthand experience in Banning proved to be an enormous intellectual advantage in later life. Getting my Ph.D. in western American history at Yale, I learned the standing models of the field, most of them derived from Frederick Jackson Turner's frontier thesis. At long last, I had to ask the key question: Did these models and theories of western American development have *anything* to do with Banning, with a life I remembered in a place that certainly seemed to be the real West?

The disorienting answer to the question was a solid ''no.'' Drawing a picture of white Americans sequentially meeting and taming wilderness as the frontier line moved west, Turner had conspicuously left out Banning, and the many western communities like it. A cat named Cabrillo, a friend named Aquilino Diano Eusebio Antonio Sapaden, a visit to the Russian colony at Fort Ross—none of this could fit anywhere in the Turner Thesis. It took several years, but I finally had to trust the concrete evidence of my own western experience, and to reject the abstract theorizing of Turner and his followers. And that decision led to the writing of a book called *The Legacy of Conquest: The Unbroken Past of the American West,* countering the old frontier school with a genuinely multicultural model and generally pepping up the discourse surrounding western American history.

The image of our poor Sunday school teacher, shaken to her toes by our undiplomatic inquiry into the meaning of key ethnic terms, provides an important glimpse of the paradox of western American history. Residents of the region with the most cosmopolitan history in the nation, we are nonetheless perennially surprised by the presence of all these ''others.'' For centuries, the basic theme of western American history has been the convergence of diverse people, encounters among people of wildly different backgrounds. When Lee Sapaden and I sat amiably next to each other at graduation in Banning, one of those wildly improbable and yet fully taken-for-granted meetings took place. One chain of events led back to the founding of the Mormon church in New York in 1830, the selection of Utah as the Latter-day Saints' homeland, and the dispatching of Mormon missionaries to Scandinavia, while another chain of events led back to the Spanish conquest of the Philippines, the American defeat of Spain in 1898, the American crushing of the Philippine ''rebellion,'' and the pull of opportunity that the labor demands of the West Coast exerted on the Asian side of the Pacific Rim. Encounters at this level of improbability have been daily fare in western America for centuries. This region has, everyone knows, perfectly astonishing physical landscapes. But the network of ties and encounters between humans adds up to a social landscape that can make the region's geography look plain and predictable by comparison. Understanding this remarkable human diversity requires a new way of thinking about both the past and the present: a rendezvous model of western America.

THE RENDEZVOUS MODEL OF WESTERN HISTORY

If the explorer John C. Fremont had lived in the late twentieth century, he would not have won awards for sensitivity. Exploring the Far West in the 1840s, Fremont put himself forward as the embodiment of Anglo-American courage and enterprise. And yet, for all his faith in the superior destiny of white Americans, Fremont was fully aware of the ethnic diversity already established in the West. Traveling east from Southern California in 1844, he described the striking appearance of his exploring party: "guided by a civilized Indian, attended by two wild ones from the Sierra; a Chinook from the Columbia; and our own mixture of American, French, German . . . ; four or five languages heard at once; . . . American, Spanish, and Indian dresses intermingled—such was our composition." The party also included Jacob Dodson, "a free young colored man of Washington city, who . . . performed his duty manfully throughout the voyage."

Fremont's description of the ethnic mosaic of his party presents a compelling case study in the rendezvous model. In its application to the West, the term originated in the annual meeting held in the 1820s and 1830s at the peak of the Rocky Mountain fur trade. Merchants brought trade goods from Missouri to a selected site in the Rockies, and a diverse crowd converged to exchange furs for commodities that were otherwise hard to come by in mountain life. Indian people from a variety of tribes, French Canadians, Irishmen, Scots, Germans, Mexicans, and white Americans came together at the rendezvous. They came, literally, from all directions. In the midst of the lively and sometimes disorderly exchanges of a rendezvous, the traditional idea of a frontier line moving steadily from east to west was an abstraction with no connection to reality.

Put the idea of the rendezvous in the place of the old model of the westward-moving frontier, and western American history gains new, and deeper, meaning. The idea of the frontier—a line of encounter where civilization met savagery or, alternatively, where white English-speaking

Americans met "the others"—was stretched to the point of snapping by the complex human reality of the American West. The idea of the rendezvous, however, has flexibility built into it; using it as a model, the American West comes forward in its true colors as one of the great meeting grounds of the planet, a region where representatives of Indian America, Latin America, Europe, Africa, and Asia continue to meet.

This image of the American West as a great meeting ground was a perfectly familiar idea to alert observers of the region in the nineteenth century. Sailing along the Pacific Northwest coast in search of furs for the China trade, American seamen encountered English, Russian, French, and Spanish sailors in the same waters. In Hawaii, in the years following the arrival of Captain James Cook in 1778, Hawaiian natives watched the accumulation of a small group of beachcombers of English, American, Irish, Portuguese, and Genoese backgrounds. On their journey to the Oregon coast, Lewis and Clark drew on the river-running talents of French Canadians, relied on Indians for guidance, horses, and food, and traveled in company with a popular and forceful black man named York. Engaged in the Santa Fe trade, American merchants recognized that Hispanos had a long history of residence in New Mexico, and that Pueblo Indians had an even longer one. Anglo-Americans on the Overland Trail were struck and, often enough, charmed by the Indian people they met during the journey. "In short, my only happiness on the plains," wrote one remarkable fellow, "were my meetings with Indians." In a similar spirit, Polly Coon, an overland traveler in 1852, recorded her own changed feelings: "We have been visited by many Indians today traded some with them, hard bread for Moccasins & beads They seem perfectly friendly & kind. our fears of Indians have all disappeared."

Surely wars between whites and Indians played a major part in western history, but the violence should not keep us from paying proper attention to the amiability of many of these encounters between strangers.

Collecting cattle hides on the Southern California beach in the 1830s, Richard Henry Dana noted the diversity of his co-workers:

We had . . . representatives from almost every nation under the sun—two Englishmen, three Yankees, two Scotchmen, two Welshmen, one Irishman, three Frenchmen (two of whom were Normans, and the third from Gascony), one Dutchman, one Austrian, two or three Spaniards (from old Spain), half a dozen Spanish Americans and half-breeds, two native Indians from Chile and the island of Chiloe, one Negro, one mulatto, about twenty Italians, from all parts of Italy, as many more Sandwich Islanders, one Tahitian, and one Kanaka from the Marquesas Islands.

Rather than finding this hodgepodge irritating, Dana and his companions seemed to find it a pleasant challenge: ''amid the Babel of English, Spanish, French, Indian, and Kanaka,'' he wrote, ''we found some words that we could understand in common.''

This vision of a cosmopolitan West was by no means unique to California. ''It is seldom that such a variety of ingredients are found mixed in so small a compass,'' the Santa Fe trader Josiah Gregg reported of his companions on the trail to New Mexico in the 1830s and 1840s. ''Here were the representatives of seven distinct nations, each speaking his own native language, which produced at times a very respectable jumble of discordant sounds.'' Henry Villard, observing the scene in 1859 at the Colorado gold rush, recorded a similar impression: ''There was no want of human elements on Cherry Creek in those days. Anglo-Americans, Germans, Frenchmen, Irishmen, Mexicans, Indians—all figured there in large numbers.''

The rendezvous model of western history would not have surprised these hide-gatherers, sailors, explorers, merchants, overland emigrants, journalists, and adventurers. They had come face to face with the ethnic diversity of the West, and a surprising number of them had found that diversity acceptable, and even enjoyable. It took several intervening generations of historians, novelists, artists, and filmmakers to flatten out this story. Reducing the technicolor to monochrome, traditional American historians made the westward movement of white people the center of the story. The prior presence and later migrations of Indians, the northward movement of Spanish and Mexicans, the eastward movement of Asians and Polynesians, the southwestern movement of French Canadians, the southeastern movement of Russians—all these interesting and important currents of human activity got only the leftovers of historical attention. In the dominant "frontier" interpretation of western American history, the stars of the story were northern Europeans and white Americans, and all the others were jumbled together into an unilluminating category, "the other side of the frontier." What had been, in fact, a multi-sided convergence of people from all over the planet went on record in both the history books and the movies as a two-sided frontier: with the white civilizers from the eastern United States on one side, and, on the other, everybody else—Indians, Hispanics, French Canadians, Russians, Asians, and Polynesians.

Certainly there were ethical problems with this over-accenting of Anglo-Americans, but there were also fundamental problems of inaccuracy and dullness. Reading western history according to the frontier model was a bit like reading Shakespeare in an edited version allowing only one character per play: Caesar would be on his own, with no assassins, no wife above or below reproach, no Marc Anthony to speak at the funeral; Macbeth would live a calm and uneventful life, with no witches, no scheming wife, and no murder to haunt him.

These stories would, to put it mildly, suffer from these reductions, just as the story of western America did when the cast of characters contracted to fit the tight, polarized categories of the frontier. Not only did the stories of the western past lose drama, the West lost much of its legitimate claim to national significance. Mention "immigration," and most Americans think immediately of the northeastern United States at the turn of the century. Mention "race relations," and most Americans think instantly of the South and its conflicts between blacks and whites. Lost in those associations is the fact that the West shared in those issues, with blacks long active in the region, and with a full complement of European immigrants represented in both the western countryside and in cities. Moreover, with the presence of many diverse Indian tribes (some of them refugees from the eastern United States), with long-term Spanish settlements, and continued immigration over the Mexican border, and with a Pacific Basin coastline hooking the West into Asian trade and immigration, the West secured its status as the nation's most cosmopolitan region.

Reading western history according to the frontier model was a bit like reading Shakespeare in an edited version allowing only one character per play . . .

41

The state of Hawaii alone should give western race relations a prominent place in any survey of the topic. It was not simply that Hawaii was well-placed by geography to be a meeting point. Intent on putting together a reliable labor force, Hawaiian planters recruited Chinese, Portuguese, Japanese, Puerto Rican, Filipino, German, Scandinavian, and Korean workers. With Hawaiian natives and mainland Caucasians and blacks, Hawaii's population thus had an extraordinary range. As demographer Eleanor C. Nordyke has pointed out, in Hawaii, "all racial groups are minorities"; "the majority of the population has roots in the Pacific Islands or Asia instead of Europe or Africa"; and the white American has the instructive and valuable experience of being, on occasion, the odd man or woman out.

Hawaii may have accumulated the widest range of human population, but its general pattern was by no means atypical of the American West in general. In race relations, the West could make the turn-of-the-century northeastern urban confrontation between European immigrants and American nativists look like a family reunion. Similarly, in the diversity of languages, religions, and cultures, the West surpassed the South.

This diversity clearly presented potential for conflict, as well as cooperation. When the heterogeneous participants in the far western fur trade met at the annual rendezvous, they did considerably more fraternizing than fighting. Interpreters were on hand to cross language barriers, and the shared interest in commerce provided a common ground. And yet conflict was also part of the scene, as companies competed for turf and for skilled workers, as individual personalities clashed, and as full battles erupted between Indians and whites (though often with whites benefiting from the support of Indian allies from different tribes). The rendezvous of 1832 ended with the Battle of Pierre's Hole. When a group of trappers, leaving the rendezvous, encountered a large party of Blackfeet, the meeting got off to an immediate bad start. As one man described it, the two men who went ahead to meet the approaching Indians were "one a half-breed Iroquois, the other a Flathead Indian, who had wrongs of their own to avenge, and they never let slip a chance of killing a Blackfoot."

These two men rode forth alone to meet the enemy, as if to hold a "talk" with the principal chief who advanced to meet them, bearing the pipe of peace. When the chief extended his hand, [Antoin] Godin, the half-breed, took it, but at the same moment he ordered the Flathead to fire, and the chief fell dead.

The Blackfeet took cover in an improvised fort, and reinforcements from the rendezvous—a mixed force of whites and Flathead and Nez Perce Indians—rode in to join the battle. After a day's fighting, the site of the fort was, Nathaniel Wyeth reported, "a sickening scene of confusion and Blood."

An event that must be placed in the larger context of struggles over turf among trappers and tribes, the Battle of Pierre's Hole provides a valuable reminder that the rendezvous model contains tragedy as well as harmony, bitter economic rivalry as well as cooperation, exchanges of violence as well as exchanges of ideas. The rendezvous model cannot present a picture which is always pretty and appealing, but it does provide a sturdy, resilient, and necessary way of thinking about the West of the past, present, and future, and an important corrective to simpler, less realistic models of the West.

Use the word westerners now, and white men on handsome horses, men in equally handsome boots and hats, come to most listeners' minds. The image and reality of the cowboy will remain an important part of the region's identity. Nonetheless, it is time to give the word westerners its full range and wealth of meaning. Accurately defined, the term embraces Indians and Anglos, Hispanics and Asians, Germans and Greeks, blacks and Polynesians. The region we live in today is the world made by their meeting.

BEFORE THE ANGLOS: INDIAN, SPANISH, FRENCH, AND RUSSIANS

Europeans had barely arrived in the New World before they fell into errors represented by the term *Indian*. The phrase only recorded Columbus's error in thinking he had reached the Indies. The term was certainly not one that the natives of the Western Hemisphere used for themselves; in a variety of languages, they were inclined to call them-selves "the people." But once unleashed, the idea of "the Indian," used in the singular, as if there were one standard character involved, showed a remarkable power to flatten reality. In western America, the differences between sedentary, farming Pueblo Indians, and nomadic, buffalo-hunting Plains Indians following an annual cycle of migrations, would seem to have had the power to shake the term *Indian* permanently into pieces. The people of the Northwest coast, making their living by maritime hunting and fishing, could hardly be confused with the hunting and gathering people of the desert Great Basin. In this way and many others, western American natives made it clear that the phrase "the Indian" only makes sense if you stand at a great distance and squint at people whose individual features and customs you cannot make out.

Distinctive in their languages, economies, religions, and habits, Indian groups had their own set of conflicts and rivalries. When white people entered the picture, Indians would often put them to use as playing pieces in ongoing dramas of intertribal relations. In those terms, it was hardly surprising that groups like the Pawnee or Crow would volunteer as scouts or auxiliaries in army campaigns against the expansionist Lakota (or Sioux).

Far from waiting for the arrival of white people, prehistorically frozen in their traditional territories, the natives filled North America with a swirl of activity. Indian America had a network of trails for trade, trails for hunting, trails for religious pilgrimages, trails for general sociability. By the nineteenth century, white Americans were inclined to find Indian people who had adopted Euro-American trade goods or customs to be somehow impure, not really Indian anymore. In fact, Indian people had been trading and borrowing customs and commodities for centuries; the idea of an era of pristine and unchanging purity in the prehistoric past was a fantasy concocted in Euro-American minds.

Europeans coming into the New World entered a populated, complicated world, not an empty, virgin land. Shipwrecked on the Texas coast in 1528, the first European group to travel in what would become the western United States certainly recognized that "empty space" was not the appropriate description for this land. Relying on Indians for food and directions, Alvar Nuñez Cabeza de Vaca led a small group, including one black man, west and south to the Spanish settlements in Mexico. A permanent Spanish presence came with the creation of a colony in New Mexico in 1598. Expelled from New Mexico in the 1680 Pueblo Revolt, the Spanish returned fourteen years later. By 1821, the year of Mexican independence, a broad band of Spanish settlements stretched from Texas to California.

With comparatively few Spanish women emigrating to the New World and with a great deal of intermarriage between natives and colonizers, the Mexican population emerged as a mestizo population, genuinely a new people of mixed European, Indian, and sometimes African heritage. In places like New Mexico, remote from the centers of power in the empire, new folk cultures could evolve, blending Spanish culture and Catholicism with native traditions.

Another process of exchange was under way far to the north, as colonists in New France worked out the partnerships with Indian people that would form the core of the Canadian fur trade. Using Quebec and Montreal as their base, French traders used rivers and lakes to travel far into the interior. Intermarriage between French traders and Indian women brought into being a new people, the metis, of mixed native and European backgrounds.

Frenchmen traveled the length of the Mississippi and took the first steps of travel toward the Great Plains, while English colonists remained closely anchored to the Atlantic Coast. In 1724, a Frenchman, Etienne de Veniard, sieur de Bourgmont, led an expedition onto the Plains, as far as present-day Kansas, to meet with the Padoucas (Plains Apaches). Bourgmont's hope was to open up the interior for trade by persuading the Padoucas to permit Frenchmen a free passage through to the Spanish settlements in New Mexico. "When the French come to see us," the Padouca chief said agreeably, "we shall welcome them, and if they should wish to go to the Spaniards to trade, we will take them there," and then invited the Frenchmen to a feast. Bourgmont never returned, and other Indians displaced the Padoucas from their pivotal location, but October of 1724 marked an amiable cross-cultural meeting in the middle of the continent.

While Frenchmen and Indians toasted each other in Kansas, a pro-

When white people entered the picture, Indians would often put them to use as playing pieces in ongoing dramas of intertribal relations.

45

cess that would lead to a different kind of encounter was under way with the eastward expansion of Russia through Siberia and toward Alaska. In 1784, Russians established a permanent trading post on Kodiak Island. Consolidated in 1799 as the Russian-American Company, the operation immersed itself in full-speed-ahead exploitation of the fur-bearing marine life and of the hunting skills of the natives. With the intermarriage of Russian men and native women, a new population of creoles with mixed parentage joined the picture of western diversity.

By 1812, the Russian-American Company had a colony at Fort Ross in northern California, an unsuccessful attempt to establish a grain-producing outpost to feed the always-hungry base in Alaska. Transitory in some ways, the Russian settlement in California left distinct traces. Years later, researchers found that Indian people in the area of Fort Ross used Russian words for terms like *milk, boy, girl, key, greeting, I do not know anything, gun powder, tobacco, wine, wheat, corn, hops, apple, cat, spoon, nose, socks,* and *sheep,* along with modified versions of the Russian words for *vodka* and *fur.*

Russians in Alaska and California; Spanish in New Mexico, Arizona, California, and Texas; Frenchmen in Canada and along the Plains rivers; and Indians everywhere: all this activity made Anglo-Americans entering this scene something closer to "late arrivals" than "discoverers." In 1805, close to completing their trip to the Pacific, Lewis and Clark could gauge how close they were to the coast by the presence, among the Indians, of European trade goods. In the 1840s, the Canadian artist Paul Kane met Chinook Indians in the Pacific Northwest who greeted him with the phrase "clak-hoh-ah-yah," which evidently originated "in their having heard in the early days of the fur trade a gentleman named Clark frequently addressed by his friends, 'Clark, how are you?' This salutation is now applied to every white man . . . " As this example showed, the people of the Northwest had created a trade language, assembled from English, French, and various Indian languages. The Chinook dialect was a literal, linguistic embodiment of the "rendezvous model" of western history, and "clak-hoh-ah-yah" was a reminder that what the mythmakers would call the "pristine wilderness" was, by the 1840s, already a land much transformed by the great rendezvous of western history.

THE RUSH OF MINING: THE RENDEZVOUS ACCELERATES

A German Swiss immigrant, John Augustus Sutter arrived in Mexican California in 1839, and soon secured a sizable land grant, the colony of New Helvetia. Employed by Sutter, John Marshall was doing his part for the development of the enterprise by building a timber mill, when his crew discovered gold, and unleashed on California an international flood of gold seekers. One of the first victims of the flood was Sutter himself, besieged by squatters and trespassers with little respect for the Swiss colony-founder's earlier claim.

Ideals of hardy western individualism and self-reliance aside, in California during the gold rush, cooperation helped. It was not simply that men falling prey to illness or injury, far from their families, relied on the kindness of strangers. Gold mining worked better for teams. When it came to redirecting a stream in order to get at the streambed, or shoveling gold-bearing dirt into the cradle that would rock and sift it, individualism reached its limits fast. Accordingly, men formed partnerships—and a number of those partnerships added new dimensions to the rendezvous model. In defiance of the standing prejudices of the time, a number of those partnerships involved cooperation between blacks and whites. A Scotsman in California, William Downie, founder of Downieville, began his enterprise with a party of nine men, seven of them black—a partnership formed "when several Negro miners who had been working the river nearby dropped into Downie's store for a drink." Anti-black prejudice was certainly present in the California placer mines, but a surprising degree of cooperation also came into play.

The news of gold spread in all directions, attracting not only white Americans and black Americans, but also Indians, Hispanic Californians, Mexicans, South Americans, various Europeans, Australians, and Chinese. It would go against human nature to expect such an encounter to be a universally happy one, especially when competition for riches provided the occasion of the meeting. With astonishing speed, white Americans who had barely set foot in California—a territory transferred to American ownership only in 1848— rearranged the terms of *foreigner* and *native,* taking the role of legitimate possessors of California for themselves, and assigning the role of "foreigner" to the others.

Anti-Asian feelings, in particular, took root in California and then spread eastward with the spread of mining. In 1879, the British writer Robert Louis Stevenson rode an emigrant railroad car across the continent and reflected on the anti-Chinese sentiment he encountered. "Of all stupid ill-feelings," Stevenson said bluntly, "the sentiment of my fellow-Caucasians towards our companions in the Chinese car was the most stupid and the worst. They seemed never to have looked at them, or thought of them, but hated them *a priori.*" Stevenson himself took another view: "For my own part I could not look but with wonder and respect on the Chinese. Their forefathers watched the stars before mine had begun to keep pigs. Gunpowder and printing, which the other day we imitated, and a school of manners which we never had the delicacy so much as to desire to imitate, were theirs in a long-past antiquity."

To Stevenson, a railroad train carrying immigrants from both Europe and China represented a key turning point in world history: "Hungry Europe and hungry China, each pouring from their gates in search of provender, had here come face to face. The two waves had met; . . . the whole round world had been prospected . . . ; there was no El Dorado anywhere; and till one could emigrate to the moon, it seemed as well to stay patiently at home." In Stevenson's mind, the meeting of Asia and Europe in the American West provided an international occasion for sobering up from the rush of empire-building, for assessing one's own long-term resources, for revitalizing the idea of a permanent home. "It seems to me," he wrote, " . . . as if this railway were the one typical achievement of the age on which we live, as if it brought together into one plot all the ends of the world. . . . "

Robert Louis Stevenson was hardly the representative voice of his time. Any number of Europeans and Euro-Americans would have been completely puzzled, and even angered, by his reflections. Appraising the swirl of populations in western America, Stevenson proved the unpredictability and variety of human thought. Looking at prejudice and racism in the regional past, some historians are inclined to the men-of-their-times school of thought, to the notion that white people of the time all thought alike, as if their thoughts and sentiments had been poured into the same molds, with their worldviews cast into interchangeable parts. Intended to defend the people of the past against criticism or judgment, the men-of-their-times argument in fact does the people of the past a grave disservice, flattening out the distinctiveness and variety of their minds.

Some western white people in the nineteenth century were captives to bitterness and hatred; and some found racial bitterness to be a trap they did not choose to enter. This second category included a wide range of people who were not, like Stevenson, "outside" intellectuals. Settling in Washington in the 1850s, Phoebe Goodell Judson took pleasure in learning the Chinook jargon from an old Indian man, denounced the execution of the leaders of the Indian rebellions of the 1850s ("Capital punishment is a relic of barbarism and a disgrace to every civilized nation that upholds it," she wrote), and adopted a number of children from mixed Indian-white marriages. The argument that leaders of anti-Indian, anti-Chinese, anti-Hispanic, or anti-black movements were simply "men of their times" must take into account the existence of "people of their times" like Mrs. Judson.

UNLIKELY NEIGHBORS

Within six years of each other, two girls—one Russian Jew, one American black—came with their families to homestead in North Dakota. Fleeing the persecution of Jews in czarist Russia, Sophie Trupin's family came to farm outside Wilton, North Dakota, in 1908. Originally from Virginia, Era Bell Thompson's parents moved to Iowa, and then to Driscoll, North Dakota, in 1914. The "closest neighbors" of Sophie Trupin's family were "also Jewish homesteaders"; in 1914, responding to the news of war in Europe, neighbors and friends gathered at Sophie's house, and while "all spoke Yiddish," each "had a different way of pronouncing the same words" since they "came from Russia, Poland, Roumania, and Hungary." Era Bell Thompson's family found fewer people of similar background; at one Christmas gathering, shared with the Williams family, "there were," she remembered, "fifteen of us, four percent of the state's entire Negro population." Their distinctive background aside, they were by no means isolated. The Olsons, a Norwegian man, who spoke "broken English," and his Scotch wife, formed "a strong and lasting friendship'' with Era Bell's parents; another family of northern European origins, the Nordlands, ''felt close to us,'' she remembered, ''for they, too, had come from Iowa''; and a German widower, Carl Brendel, brought the family food when crop failure left them destitute.

Both Sophie and Era Bell had their encounters with prejudice. ''I remember only one overtly anti-Semitic incident,'' Sophie wrote, when a little girl ''picked up a stick and flung it, barely missing me. As she did this she screwed up her face and hissed at me, 'Christ killer!' '' But emigration had changed the whole tenor of Sophie's response: ''This was not czarist Russia; we were not hiding in the attic. We were in America, and this was just a stupid little girl.'' Era Bell Thompson also had a run-in or two with bigots. Attending school in Sterling, she remembered that ''the children stared the first day or two, some of the boys called me 'nigger,' but I didn't chase them, didn't cry, so they gave it up, because it wasn't any fun that way. And when they found that I could run faster, push the swings higher than most of them, I had many friends.''

While black Americans and Russian Jews formed a small percentage of the North Dakota population, settlers with origins in unlikely places were more the rule than the exception. A recent book, *Plains Folk: North Dakota's Ethnic History,* describes people of the British Isles, Germans of both western and eastern European origins, Scandinavians, and Slavic peoples, and smaller groups of Japanese, Chinese, Italians, Armenians, Greeks, Syrians, Dutch, French, Belgians, Gypsies, blacks, Jews, Spaniards and Mexicans. The state kept, as well, a significant proportion of Indian people. Moving to North Dakota, Era Bell Thompson and Sophie Trupin not only encountered a novel world of nature, they entered a novel world of human nature as well.

While her mother defied the obstacles to tradition and continued to keep a kosher house, Sophie Trupin's life was an ongoing language school. ''In my home I heard three, and sometimes four languages every day. My parents continued to speak Yiddish to us, and we answered in Yiddish. Hebrew was reserved for prayer, and this we heard every day. . . . My father used [Russian] when he was especially frustrated with the animals, or when something went wrong with the machinery.'' Meanwhile, Era Bell taught some neighboring German boys ''to shoot gophers and tin cans with a .22,'' while they taught her ''how to swear in German.'' Later, after her mother's death, Era Bell moved to Bismarck, North Dakota, where her best friend was Jewish. ''Occasionally Sarah and I wandered into enemy territory, neighborhoods where the kids called us names,'' she remembered; ''but if they called me a coon, they called her a kike,'' and neither girl had to feel embarrassed in front of the other.

The centuries had changed over; the twentieth-century West had succeeded the nineteenth-century West; and the rendezvous went on. Lines of friendship, as well as lines of friction, continued to tie people of vastly different origins into the same story. In the coal towns of southern Wyoming, miners from southern Europe brought in ''carloads of grapes'' and made wine in their homes. Hugh Crouch, a black miner, remembered the sociability that accompanied this home industry: ''When we wasn't making it, we had Italian people that always at Christmas would have us to come over and get us a Christmas drink and give us a gallon or two of wine. I had one neighbor [who] I had to drink wine with every evening when we came home from work. Come on over before we should take a bath. Get the coal dust out of our throats.''

It was a scene that one would never see in classic western movies: Italian and black miners getting together for socializing. But the scene stood for the well-established pattern of western American life: of improbable meetings, and often enough, surprising amiability. In the 1970s, immigration from Asia widened, adding Vietnamese, Cambodians, and Hmong, to the already diverse groups of Chinese, Japanese, and Koreans. A Vietnamese immigrant in California testified to the persistence of the rendezvous model in an urban setting. ''Sometimes I meet the mother-in-law [of his Mexican-American neighbor],'' he reported, ''and I try to speak Spanish with her, since that is the only language she knows. She is from Mexico. She likes it when I speak with her. She is friendly. We talk about where we have come from, how many children she has. . . . '' Another Vietnamese immigrant recorded an even more improbable friendship: ''Another neighbor, an American Indian, also likes us very much. When he and his family went to the Philippines, we watched their house. When they came home, they gave us a gift bought in the Philippines. They know we are good people, so they trust us. I drove them to the

Lines of friendship, as well as lines of friction, continued to tie people of vastly different origins into the same story.

51

airport and brought their car back home. When they returned, I picked them up at the airport. So we have a very good friendship.''

Friendships tying Vietnamese immigrants to Mexican-Americans and to American Indians give a remarkably happy impression of the great western rendezvous. But the other strain—of prejudice, injury, oppression, and exploitation—remains a part of the story in the twentieth century. Anglo-American contempt for and exclusion of people of color continued to show itself in hundreds of cases: from indifference to the Indian struggle with unemployment and demoralization, to alarm over the speaking of Spanish in areas of the West first settled by Hispanics; from the internment of Japanese-Americans in World War II to housing discrimination against blacks in many western cities.

Prejudice and injustice were not, however, weapons designed for the exclusive use of Anglo-Americans. In his autobiography, *America Is in the Heart,* the Filipino immigrant Carlos Bulosan recorded many encounters with Anglo-American prejudice. But he also recorded the advice of a Filipino friend, explaining life in California to him: ''The Chinese syndicates, the gambling lords, are sucking the blood of our people. The [Filipinos] work every day in the fields but when the season is over their money is in the Chinese vaults!'' The pattern went beyond representatives of one ethnic group preying on representatives of another. Newly arrived in the United States, Bulosan had immediately fallen into the hands of Filipino labor contractors, who took advantage of his poverty to send him off to work in the Alaskan fish canneries, skimming their commission from the transaction.

This was an extremely common pattern in the life of minorities. Chinese, Japanese, Filipino, Mexican, Italian, or Greek, newly arrived workers were vulnerable to manipulation by countrymen who knew English and the American system and who thus wielded considerable power over their fellows. In Utah, Greek immigrants formed a significant part of the mining labor force, and, as the historian Helen Zeese Papanikolas reports, ''many beatings and killings among early Greeks that baffled the authorities were the revenge of laborers for the cruel acts of interpreters and of labor agents.'' In Hawaii, a Japanese folk verse recorded workers' hostility to the chief inspector of the Japanese section of the Hawaii Bureau of Immigration, a man named Joji Nakayama, who exploited his powers for personal profit:

> *The workers keep on coming*
> *Overflowing these Islands.*
> *But it's only middleman Nakayama*
> *Who rakes in the money.*

The force of ethnic solidarity and personal profit often collided with each other, leaving us with no clear modern-day arrangement of white hats and black hats, good guys and bad guys.

No group in western America escaped the basic workings of human nature. While prejudice from outside, or the general disorientation of new surroundings, could unite a group on the basis of shared nationality, no community lived a life of unbroken internal harmony. No group held a monopoly on cruelty, just as no group enjoyed a monopoly on virtue. It was perfectly possible to be exploited, victimized, or oppressed, and then, in turn, to exploit, victimize, or oppress others. The widely distributed capacity to treat others as objects is, if anything, only more evidence that we are indeed, in the phrase of the western journalist and humanitarian Carey McWilliams, "brothers"—and sisters—"under the skin."

APPRAISING THE RENDEZVOUS

Western America has, for centuries, been home to an extravagant range of cultures, religions, and languages. That part is settled fact; the questions come when we ask ourselves how we should react to this fact, how we should appraise it, how we should *value* it. To the western American historian, the answer is easy: the diversity of the region is a fact to be celebrated because it makes for a far more interesting story. The improbability of this cast of characters exceeds anything that the free imagination of fiction writers could create. The spread of perspectives and points of view presents a constant intellectual puzzle that one never quite masters. The region's human diversity is the only genuinely infinite resource, an unending treasure trove of stories and lessons and challenges to the understanding.

Not everyone has enjoyed the luxury and tranquility of the historian's point of view. Other westerners, caught in a scramble for scarce resources or a struggle for jobs, have been inclined to see western ethnic diversity as a problem, rather than an opportunity. When white workingmen in California in the 1870s felt unrewarded in their labor, let down by the promise of the California dream, it was their instinct to blame their problems on Chinese immigrants, and to see the solution to those problems in the prohibition of Chinese labor. Scapegoating is a mental habit to which the human mind takes easily, and the patterns of western American economic development have left many vulnerable to that temptation. The American West was cast as the land of promise and opportunity; people arriving with such high expectations ran a considerable risk of disappointment. When that disappointment hit, it was a natural temptation to find someone to blame, to take up an "us versus them" worldview and to direct resentment toward the "foreigners." White westerners not only imported a full share of traditional Anglo-American pride and prejudice, they then encountered circumstances—of economic frustration, of bewilderment at the range of human character—that gave both pride and prejudice a new, defensive edge.

But even the most determined racists found that the reality of the western population put a strain on their rigid categorization of humanity. White Americans with a firm conviction that whites were superior to blacks found that this simple proposition could not provide much guidance in the multi-ethnic West. If whites outranked blacks, then where did Indians fit? Were some tribes better than others? Were Hispanics entitled to a higher rung in the hierarchy because of their European heritage, or would they be assigned to a lower rung because of their mixed ancestry? Were Asians superior, or inferior, to Hispanics, Indians, and blacks? Should there be separate and distinct rankings for Chinese, Japanese, Korean, and Filipino people? And if all this could be sorted out, would there be any energy left for scorning the Irish, or the southern and eastern Europeans, or would the common ground of European origins make them more tolerable than these "others"?

Applied to the West, racism demanded an extra investment of time and energy. Eventually the question would have to be faced: was it worth the trouble? The region's diversity put a spotlight on the arbitrariness of racial hierarchies, exposing the shallowness of these separations and divisions. Keeping these categories spruced up and airtight was a constant work of maintenance and, finally, not a very productive use of time. Eventually examples set by others—the interpreters, mediators, cooperators, and coalition builders of western history—would begin to look not only more ethical, but more sensible and productive.

In the late nineteenth century, an army surgeon named Bernard James Byrne arrived in Santa Fe, began to feel disoriented, and, at first, responded with irritation. "As I walked along the street," he wrote, "I stopped several citizens to ask the way. No one could speak English; the answer to each question was *'Quien sabe.'*" Byrne's temper began to wear thin: "I finally got indignant to think of walking a street in my own country and not being able to find a citizen who spoke the language, but I cooled off when I reflected that Indians and Mexicans had been here ages before I was; I was the interloper."

The name Bernard James Byrne is hardly a household word, having been solidly eclipsed by Billy the Kid and George Armstrong Custer and Wild Bill Hickok. But his thoughtfulness and tolerance are both important components of the western American heritage. Three decades before him, the overland traveler Edwin Bryant met a young Indian man mid-journey; he was "about twenty-five, with an amiable but sprightly expression of countenance." Bryant found him "so eager and earnest in his inquiries respecting every thing appertaining to us, and into our language, that I sat conversing with him until a late hour of the night. From him, I learned the names of many things in the Utah dialect."

More than two centuries before Bryant and his Indian acquaintance had their conversation, a scientist named Georg Wilhelm Steller had yearned for exactly that kind of exchange. Originally from Germany, Steller had made his career in Russia. Sailing with the Vitus Bering expedition of 1741 to find and explore Alaska, Steller had great hopes of meeting, and learning from, American natives. But the officers in charge of the expedition barely set foot on North America, beginning a retreat while Steller was still eager to press ahead. A brief encounter with the "Americans" took a turn to hostility when the natives wanted their visitors to stay and the visitors undertook to depart, with force. "[We] returned rather displeased to the packet boat," Steller wrote, "because we could not observe what we wished, but had, on the contrary, encountered what we had not expected."

Unlike Steller, Edwin Bryant got what he wanted in the way of cross-cultural exchange. To Bryant and his Indian acquaintance, the fascination of human variety overcame distrust, caution, and the barriers of language. The free flow of their curiosity, matched with their willingness to answer each other's questions, even when those questions reflected a laughable ignorance, serves well as an example of the kinds of exchanges and conversations we are still in need of, if we are to know our neighbors. We live, today, with an abundant supply of the opportunities to converse that men like Georg Wilhelm Steller yearned for, and could not secure.

Writing of her life on a North Dakota farm, the Russian Jewish homesteader Sophie Trupin reflected on the key term *neighbor*: "It's difficult to define what the word *neighbor* meant in the days I'm writing about. It was more than just a relationship . . . Although these people were courageous and resourceful, they were more or less dependent upon each other."

Our circumstances, as westerners in the late twentieth century, are certainly very different from the conditions of life on a homestead seventy-five years ago, and yet the definition of the term *neighbor,* and the relation of mutual dependence it conveys, still demand our attention. For two hundred years, the pace of change in western American history has proceeded at a dizzying rate. The populating of the region has taken place at a speed one can only call "fast forward," as Indian people have watched enormous numbers of strangers, starting from virtually every point on the planet, descend on their homeland. This rush of population has left the people in the region in a persistent state of perplexity as to who "belongs" here, who is a rightful resident and who is a late and unwanted invader. And yet, with the clear exception of Indian people, it is our status as immigrants and late arrivals that provides our common identity. Beginning with an arrival in strange land with strange companions, immigrants into the West have taken a psychological journey toward the status of being "at home." Moving to North Dakota as a young child, Era Bell Thompson drew on the adaptability of youth to complete that journey before her parents and her older brothers: "Of all the family," she remembered, "I alone was happy on our land, content to call it home."

For the rendezvous model, the year 1890, long treated by western historians as the end of the frontier, carried no meaning as a deadline. Far greater numbers of Americans moved to the West in the twentieth century than in the nineteenth century. In the west-to-east dimension of the rendezvous, Japanese immigration picked up after 1890; in the south-to-north dimension, Mexican immigration surged after 1910.

One participant in that south-to-north movement was the child Ernesto Galarza, who would later be a prominent American sociologist with a Ph.D. from Columbia University. As a quick-learning child in Sacramento, Galarza moved into the traditional role of interpreter, helping his fellow Mexicans in encounters with institutions like courtrooms and hospitals. "My services were not professional but they were free," he remembered, "except for the IOUs I accumulated from families who always thanked me with 'God will pay you for it.' " Opportunities for an informal translator were not difficult to come by: Galarza's neighborhood in Sacramento was a classic case study in the western American rendezvous. The "mix of many nationalities" included Japanese, Chinese, Filipinos, Hindus, Portuguese, Italians, Poles, Yugoslavs, Koreans, and blacks—"a kaleidoscope of colors and languages and customs that surprised and absorbed me at every turn." Of all these people, perhaps the most puzzling were the white Americans: "We found the Americans as strange in their customs as they probably found us," Galarza wrote. Americans had peculiar grocery stores, smelling of "fly spray and oiled floors, not of fresh pineapple and limes"; they did not have a plaza, "a place which was the middle of things for everyone." Americans roared when they laughed, and "until you got used to them you could hardly tell whether the boisterous Americans were roaring mad or roaring happy."

Ernesto Galarza reminds us that the western rendezvous has always been a multi-sided transaction, with people from a variety of origins all looking at each other's puzzling customs, and trying to figure them out.

This rush of population has left the people in the region in a persistent state of perplexity as to who "belongs" here . . .

57

In the nineteenth century, a man named Thomas Leflorge, who lived with the Crow Indians for twenty years, gave us a similar reminder. "The Indians liked to hear of the strange ways of white people," he remembered. "They wondered at these peculiarities, the same as white people wonder at the customs prevailing among Indians."

These and other examples keep us aware that the word *westerner,* contrary to the image presented in movies and ads, includes a range of people who are not necessarily tall white men, wearing cowboy hats and mounted on horses in the open plains. Westerner includes a young Mexican boy interpreting for his people in early twentieth-century Sacramento; a group of Crow Indians finding "the strange ways of white people" both puzzling and fascinating; a young black girl and a young Russian Jewish girl homesteading with their families in twentieth-century North Dakota; the Scotchman James Downie and his seven black partners in gold-rush California; the Chinese people who, in 1870, were one quarter of the population in Idaho; the Basques from Spain and France making their mark on the landscape of Idaho and Nevada with their distinctive hotels, rooming houses, and restaurants; and the representatives from various Indian and European nationalities attending the annual fur trade rendezvous, in the early nineteenth century, in the interior of western America.

In a variety of ways, these westerners have been traveling in converging journeys; their paths have crossed, whether that was the travelers' intention or not. After a century and a half of these improbable encounters, it is simply too late to find the diversity of the region to be inappropriate, unexpected, or somehow or other "not the way the West should be." The presence of people from widely different origins has been a central fact of life in western America, and there is, in the 1990s, every reason to take that spectrum as one of our region's assets, and not as a disappointing liability to be denied or evaded. History is full of people who have found the West to be the best sort of classroom, a place to learn about other people's languages, customs, and experiences, and to reach, thereby, a new appreciation of one's own opportunities in life. Those lively and curious people of the past, making the most of the chance to meet their neighbors, can indeed be our role models today.

Many westerners have also, intentionally or not, been approaching the destination Era Bell Thompson reached in North Dakota: the recognition that she was "happy on our land, content to call it home." In western American history over the last hundred and fifty years, mobility and transience have set the terms of the story, as immigrants into the region have responded to restless visions of better prospects elsewhere. But in the late twentieth century, westerners confront, on one side, the limits of extractive economies and, on the other side, the attractions of life in the distinctive physical and social environments of the region. The West seems at long last to be settling down. To many people—of a variety of ethnicities—in the nineteenth and twentieth centuries, the West was a place where treasure was hidden; one ripped the place apart to get the treasure out, and left the surrounding environment behind like Christmas wrappings with the presents removed. Now that careless approach has begun to seem shortsighted and worrisome. Many westerners— whether Indian, Hispanic, black, white, or Asian—now think of the region as the place where they themselves want to live permanently, and where they would like their descendants to live. The West is no longer an exotic place situated "out there," in some distant location in the Anglo-American imagination. The West has become, for many late-twentieth-century westerners, the home where we live, in the company of our various neighbors.

59

Gardeners at home. Hawaii. Photo © Jerry Chong.

Musical theatre production. North Dakota.
Photo © Sheldon Green.

Skokimish artist. Washington. Photo © Monty Roessel.

Eskimo artist. Anaktuuk Pass, Alaska. Photo © George Wuerthner.

Rancher. Buck Rack, Montana. Photo © George Wuerthner.

Bush Pilot. Alaska. Photo © George Wuerthner.

Little Dancer, Blackfoot Tribe. Montana. Photo © George Wuerthner.

Cowboy poets. North Dakota. Photo © Sheldon Green.

Arizona miner. Photo © Monty Roessel.

Dancers. New Mexico. Photo © Steven Meckler

TOWARD AN ETHIC OF PLACE
Charles F. Wilkinson

The making of public policy in the American West is accompanied by regular flashes of contentiousness that exceed those in any other region in the country. We can see this on many levels. Looking at the long sweep and fusion of past and present, western historians properly emphasize the region's boom-and-bust economy; the continuing quest to remake nature; and wars over range, water, Indian-white relations, and Mexican land and immigration. Those struggles live with us today. Historian Patricia Nelson Limerick has said in her brilliant book, *The Legacy of Conquest,* that:

> The history of the West is a study of a place undergoing conquest and never fully escaping its consequences. Conquest basically involved the drawing of lines on a map, the definition and allocation of ownership (personal, tribal, corporate, state, federal, and international), and the evolution of land from matter to property. The process had two stages: the initial drawing of the lines . . . and the subsequent giving of meaning and power to those lines, which is still underway. . . .
>
> The contest for property and profit has been accompanied by a contest for cultural dominance. Conquest also involved the struggle over languages, cultures and religions; the pursuit of legitimacy in property overlapped with the pursuit of legitimacy in way of life and point of view.

Lower Proxy Falls, Three Sisters Wilderness,
Oregon. Photo © George Wuerthner.

71

A person can see the essential conflict in the American West in other ways. We see it in great public issues such as the furious hearings of 1988–89 on the proposed Two Forks Dam on the South Platte River that were conducted in various Colorado Western Slope and Front Range locales and in Nebraska. We see it in the bitter, longstanding charges and countercharges among Alaska's business leaders; Natives; loggers, hunters, and fishers; and environmentalists over the state's land, oil fields, forests, wildlife, and fisheries. We see it in the zealous faces of Earth First! activists, who talk of, and maybe accomplish, the spiking of old trees in order to plant the equivalent of land mines for those who would log deep into the ancient forests; and we saw it, too, in the angry faces of the members of the grass-roots organization Women in Timber, of Dubois, Wyoming, as they struggled to save jobs in the Louisiana Pacific mill from the perceived excessive demands of local environmentalists.

The seemingly endless series of such juxtapositions has rarely created satisfactory or lasting results. Often, although not always, the dissenting parties depart angry, determined to undercut the temporary solution bred of combativeness. Perhaps worse, the process tears at our sense of community; it leaves us more a loose collection of fractious subgroups than a coherent society with common hopes and dreams.

The region's fiction also brings to life the way in which policy is made at loggerheads, by confrontation. One of Edward Abbey's early novels is *Fire on the Mountain,* in which a cantankerous old rancher, John Vogelin, holds out when the army wants to condemn his ranch and BLM grazing leases and add them to the White Sands Missile Base in New Mexico. Vogelin is a surrogate, not just for the utterly reconstructed Ed Abbey, but for a good many old-time westerners:

"The Box V is not for sale!" Grandfather thundered. . . . "The Box V is not for sale. The Box V never was for sale. The Box V never will be for sale. And by God no pack of brass hats and soldier boys and astro—astronauts or whatever you call 'em is going to take it away from me. I'll die first. No—they'll die first. Why I never heard of such a thing. Every citizen of Guadalupe County, every mother's son in New Mexico, should be loading his guns right now. . . .

"I am the land," Grandfather said. "I've been eating this dust for seventy years. Who owns who? They'll have to plow me under."

The contentiousness plays out in tragic ways that are not even remotely fictional. The *New York Times* has reported that the rates of violent death in numerous rural western communities exceed those in the inner cities of the nation's urban areas—New York, Chicago, Detroit. The *Denver Post* recently did a two-part series on an extraordinary spate of juvenile suicides—it amounts to an epidemic—that has been recurring for years in two central Wyoming towns.

I am not suggesting that these incidents, alone or in the aggregate, are representative of contemporary life in the American West. In no sense am I trying to tell the whole story of the whole West through these vignettes. But each incident is important in its own right, each is tied in a reasonably direct way to distinctive regional characteristics, and each hints at fundamental regional problems.

Let me give some examples. Boom and bust cycles are due in large part to the West's role as primary storehouse for the nation's mineral deposits. Thus, Denver's current 26-percent vacancy rate for office space traces to optimism generated by the explosive growth in the minerals industry in the late 1970s and the subsequent plummeting of demand for energy fuels. Two Forks Dam is in the front part of our consciousness because of the central role that water has always played in the Intermountain West and because of the increasing scarcity of major undammed canyons in the West. Timber disputes in Dubois and federal project development at John Vogelin's ranch near White Sands reflect the fact that 50 percent—think of it, a full half—of all land in the eleven western states is owned by the federal government. The violence in our rural towns, social scientists believe, is linked to our longtime reliance on extractive resource development, where jobs are often dangerous and where rootlessness is common. Even the outbreak of suicides is tied to distinctive regional qualities, for the victims were young Indian people, members of the Wind River Tribe in Wyoming, people who had to face the gut-ripping tug and pull between traditional ways and a larger society that at once lures them with its television glamour and spurns them

73

with its racism.

Communities in the West are younger and less rooted than any region in the country. Our towns lack the stability and sense of community found, for example, in villages in New England and the Midwest. There are exceptions to this around the West—some Montana ranch communities, pueblos along the Rio Grande, and villages on Hawaii's outer islands, rural towns in Utah come to mind—but they remain exceptions.

The problem of community divisiveness is aggravated by western laws. Two forces are at work encouraging adversarial encounters. First, a great many natural resources laws operating today have their genesis in the mid- or late-nineteenth century, a time when westerners held extreme laissez-faire attitudes toward public resources such as water, wildlife, timber, minerals, and rangeland. The legal solutions of the time reflected those attitudes; the Hardrock Mining Law of 1872 and the prior appropriation doctrine for water, both rudimentary rules of capture, are showcase examples. Somewhat similarly, nineteenth-century whites denied the humanity of Indian people and essentially saw no wrong in taking their land, their natural resources, or even their lives. Although these perceptions have changed, the laws that embody the old beliefs remain in force.

Environmentalists, in particular, have repeatedly come into collision with these antiquated laws—these lords of yesterday—and have had little choice but to engage in pitched battles that are more often directed at the outmoded laws than at the westerners who espouse them. Still, the result is personal hostility and shallow solutions, caused in part by the environmentalists' inherent difficulty in making proposals that take economic interests into account when the nineteenth-century laws, still on the statute books, are radically tilted toward extractive interests.

Another reason for policy by loggerheads is deeply ingrained in the institutional personalities of the federal agencies that make so many decisions in the West. Federal officials exacerbate policy by conflict. Taking a range of sophisticated actions, some instinctive, some intentional, they play interest groups against each other, creating the posture of an agency in the center—a compromising, reasonable, middle-road entity.

The process of achieving results through combat will not change completely, and the changes that do come will not come easily. These are inherently tough problems due to cultural differences, resource scarcity, and economic pressures. There is a certain level of contentiousness that will never entirely go away. We are not about to enter an era of immediate, deep, and permanent bonding between the drivers of Volvo station wagons sporting "Babies can't be cuddled with nuclear arms" bumper stickers and the owners of Ford pickups insured by Smith & Wesson.

Still, over time, we can ameliorate these problems. We deserve and can achieve more stable, tight-knit communities, communities bound together by the common love of this miraculous land, of this region the likes of which exists nowhere else on earth. We can do much better.

We need to develop what I call an ethic of place. It is premised on a sense of place, the recognition that our species thrives on the subtle, intangible, but soul-deep mix of landscape, smells, sounds, history, neighbors, and friends that constitute a place, a homeland. An ethic of place respects equally the people of a region and the land, animals, vegetation, water, and air. It recognizes that westerners revere their physical surroundings and that they need and deserve a stable, productive economy that is accessible to those with modest incomes. An ethic of place ought to be a shared community value and ought to manifest itself in a dogged determination to treat the environment and its people as equals, to recognize both as sacred, and to insure that all members of the community not only search for, but insist upon, solutions that fulfill the ethic.

This is a broad formulation, and like all such generalities, there is an inherent difficulty in moving it down close to the ground. But we need ethics in order to guide our conduct according to the larger considerations that ought to supersede day-to-day, short-term pressures. It is one of our special qualities as human beings that we understand spans of time, that we can learn from history, from events that occurred before our birth, and that we can conceptualize the long reach of time out in front of us. Ethics capitalize on these special human abilities and can be critical in structuring attitudes toward land and community. Further, broad policies have always mattered in the West, whether they have been Manifest Destiny, conservation, multiple use, or the Sagebrush Rebel-

Communities in the West are younger and less rooted than any region in the country.

75

lion. Such concepts provide us with points of departure in our continuing struggle to define our society and what it stands for.

It is especially necessary to identify our guideposts at this juncture in the history of the American West. Our generation has been called upon to navigate diverse and deep crosscurrents. This is evident, among many other places, in the outstanding and rapidly accumulating body of recent western fiction and nonfiction. Some of this literature raises profound questions about our relationship to the natural world. Some of it explores our social relationships. Some of it examines our regional economy, with its deep trenches and its growing insecurities for everyday rural westerners. These things need to be understood and reconciled if we are to develop an ethic of place, if we are to be what we can be.

DEVELOPING AN ETHIC OF PLACE

This ethic of place is a considerably different approach than existing concepts such as multiple use. It calls for reasonably concrete approaches to specific problems, and it has a hard edge. The ethic of place attempts to pull out the best in us but it does not purport to be all things to all people.

The most relevant boundary lines for an ethic of place in the American West accrue from basin and watershed demarcations. The region is marked off by water or, more accurately, by the lack of it. The dry line that weaves north to south between the one hundredth and ninety-eighth meridians is what Walter Prescott Webb called a "cultural fault line." West of there, people instinctively are linked to ridge lines and to the tilt of the land. It is not always easy, or necessary, to define precisely the relevant watershed—to resolve whether people living in, say, Bozeman, find definition from the Upper Missouri, the Three Forks country, or the Gallatin. The point is that Bozeman's cultural and economic identity is as likely to be perceived of in relation to one of those watersheds as it is to the state of Montana or the Upper Great Plains.

This is in no sense a suggestion that we rework our angular state lines to conform to river basins—that is not going to happen, nor would the transaction costs make it worthwhile. I suggest only that we can better understand our society by appreciating that in the West our sense of place is powerfully shaped by the course of water. This approach is linked in some degree to the emerging theory of bioregionalism, which, among other things, attempts to identify the natural geographic regions within which human beings can best assess the effects, and achieve the promise, of their work. Such a region must be the right size—small enough to understand, large enough to allow diversity and growth—and a logical configuration. If the scale is right, a watershed is an especially appropriate unit because, as Kirkpatrick Sale wrote in *Dwellers in the Land,* "a watershed—the flows and valleys of a major river system—is a particularly distinctive kind of georegion . . . with aquatic and riverine life usually quite special to that area and with human settlements and economies peculiar to that river." Residents in southeastern Wyoming surely sense some shared destiny with those Coloradans and Nebraskans living along the North Platte. In the upper Rio Grande Basin, New Mexicans and Coloradans are tied together. The Klamath River watershed makes common ground for southern Oregonians and northern Californians. On the other hand, Missoula is surely in a different community than Billings, and the same is true of Boulder and Gunnison (to which many residents of Billings and Gunnison might say "thank God").

An ethic of place looks to more things than the geography of water for definition. The legitimate governments and societies in a region must also be identified. State and local governments hold established places, as do ranching, farming, and logging communities.

We also have a great distance to go in recognizing the just place of American Indian tribes. It is one of the terrible ironies of our time that so many non-Indians see tribal rights as hypertechnical or anomalous—that they view tribal sovereignty as some convoluted fiction spun out by lawyers' trickery. In fact the legitimacy of modern tribal governments follows from pure and forceful strains of logic and history. Before contact with white societies, all the aboriginal people in the West had political organizations. Some were by tribe, others by band or clan. But all of the aboriginal tribes had legal systems: they set norms, decided disputes, and rendered punishments. Every European government, whether the English, Spanish, or French, acknowledged the existence of those governments. So did the new United States, which entered into treaties with tribal governments.

The treaties fortified tribal national existence rather than diminished it. As Chief Justice John Marshall put it, Congress "exhibited a most anxious desire to conciliate the Indian nations." Federal statutes "manifestly consider the several Indian nations as distinct political communities, having territorial boundaries, within which their authority is exclusive, and having a right to all the lands within those boundaries which is not only acknowledged, but guaranteed by the United States." The United States has not always been faithful to those guarantees as to tribal lands, but nothing has occurred to alter the political existence of Indian tribes. It has persevered for thousands of years and has been continuously acknowledged by European and American governments for no less than four centuries.

Real societies exist in Indian country. We non-Indians can go there and learn that, aided by the generosity that is the talisman of the Indian way. Or we can read of vibrant, creative tribal societies in the works of authors like Vine Deloria, Jr., James Welch, Leslie Marmon Silko, and Louise Erdrich, whose recent novel, *Love Medicine,* dealt with life on the Turtle Mountain Chippewa Reservation in North Dakota. They write candidly of poverty, unacceptable educational levels, and alcoholism—the disease that seems to hold a grudge against Indian people. But within the reservations, you will also find warmth, humor, love, and traditionalism all bound together. The smoke from the chimneys on those barren flats, as non-Indian eyes may see them, rises from fires surrounded by extended families pushing on in a changing and uncertain world as best they can, just like the rest of us. They possess individuality as people and self-rule as governments, but they are also an inseparable part of the larger community, a proud and valuable constituent group that must be extended the full measure of respect mandated by an ethic of place.

Western communities have the right to grow and prosper, and that right should be espoused by all of us. This growth should be primarily from within, activity that utilizes the talents and labor of the basin residents. We have seen development that fails to meet this ethic, that has led to well-documented charges that the rural West has been treated as a colony. In some sectors this has led to lurches in the economy and to cultural scars when the booms die out. The ethic requires that solid, stable, improving economies for the region's communities be no less important, although no more important, than a determination to respect the ground.

These human aspects are coupled with the land and animals that also exist in these places staked out by watershed boundaries. In scholarly literature, there is a sharp and enlightening debate over homocentrism (the belief that things ought to be interpreted according to human values) and biocentrism (the idea that animals and land systems have an independent right to exist entirely separate from any relationship to human beings). Why, in other words, should an animal species or a land mass be protected? Because the animals or land are inherently entitled to protection or because humans would benefit from it? Aldo Leopold, who was powerfully influenced by biocentrism, said that a land ethic would require that such things "should continue as a matter of biotic right, regardless of the presence or absence of biotic advantage to us." Several current theorists, including Bill Devall and George Sessions in the book *Deep Ecology: Living As If Nature Mattered,* argue for a biocentric approach to the environment.

Applying such thinking, of course, would have extraordinary ramifications for natural resources policy. For example, grizzly bears and wolves at the upper end of the Missouri Basin require large areas of uninhabited land for survival. Recognizing that the grizzly bears and wolves have inviolable, independent rights would stall development of even minor projects on many fronts.

An ethic of place, as I propose it, borrows from biocentric reasoning without adopting it wholesale. We should accept these and other animals as part of the community within which we live. Even if we stop short of recognizing legal rights in these animals, we should nevertheless accord them independent respect. An honest concern for their dignity and welfare ought to be one aspect of developing a policy approach toward basin management.

There are also valid homocentric reasons for a respect toward wolves and grizzly bears. In his book on free speech, *The Tolerant Society,* Lee Bollinger argues that the ultimate justification for free speech is not the

79

traditional view, that allowing self-expression by minorities furthers the search for truth. Rather, Bollinger concludes that the First Amendment makes the majority stronger by requiring of it tolerance and self-restraint. Recognition of such minority rights thus furthers "the genuine nobility of society."

Laws such as the Endangered Species Act, it follows, fulfill the ethic of place in diverse ways. The Act grants respect to the independent exist-ence and integrity of other species. The Endangered Species Act also benefits the human race, and not just by achieving pragmatic objectives such as preserving gene pools for scientific research. Such an approach pulls out the best in us and, like the First Amendment, elevates us by its proof that our unique ability to develop technology is coupled with the capacity and will to exercise a humane restraint in the name of a high calling, such as the honest respect for other species that exist with us in the same watershed. Such considerations may not always control, but such obligations to our community ought to matter profoundly to us.

The idea that an ethic of place requires respect toward other constit-uent parts of the community in no sense means that the ethic tends toward a homogeneous society. On the contrary, the ethic of place is founded on the worth of the subcultures of the West and thereby pro-motes the diversity that is the lifeblood of the region. We will always have disputes over land, water, minerals, and animals. Such raspings are inevitable and ultimately healthy in a colorful, dynamic, and individual-istic society. The overarching concern, therefore, is not to deny that conflict will occur but rather to acknowledge an ethic that sets stan-dards for resolution and, as importantly, provides a method for dealing with disputes.

Disputants need to recognize that they exist within a community and that consensus is the preferred method of resolution. Litigation is expen-sive. It is also inflexible: no judge can craft a settlement in these com-plex public disputes as well as the parties themselves. Furthermore, a voluntary agreement reached by consent draws groups into joint coop-eration during the implementation stage that follows.

It is not always possible to complete an accord at the basin level. Congress may become involved as a matter of necessity if federal funding is required or if interstate issues are substantially implicated. But even federal legislation should be the product of agreements that come from the ground up. The preferred role of Congress should be to ratify local accords among the affected elements of the basin community. For example, in the Pick-Sloan Plan of 1944, high federal agency officials divided up jurisdiction over water projects in the Missouri River Basin, the Bureau of Reclamation taking authority above Sioux City, the Army Corps of Engineers having primacy below Sioux City. Whatever its merits in its time, the Pick-Sloan Plan would be the wrong approach today because there was too much involvement by federal agencies, too little by the states, and none at all by the tribes. The proper approach toward fulfilling an ethic of place is exemplified by leaders in Washington, Oregon, Idaho, and Montana, who formulated a policy for resolving conflicts between energy production and anadromous fish protection in the Columbia River Basin. The states then presented the consensus resolution to Congress, which ratified it in the form of the Northwest Power Act of 1980.

Consensus dispute resolution involving all affected basin parties has an independent core value, one separate from the worth of ending a confrontation for the time being. An agreement can glue former adversaries together in a continuing process jointly conceived. Consensus builds trusting communities. Agreements heal and strengthen places.

Let me briefly apply the ideas behind the ethic of place to two west-wide issues and to current controversies in three watersheds.

The ethic of place is founded on the worth of the sub-cultures of the West and thereby promotes the diversity that is the lifeblood of the region.

WESTERN RANGELANDS

More acres of federal public land in the West are devoted to grazing of livestock than to any other commercial purpose. Ranchers have traditionally enjoyed great autonomy, especially on Bureau of Land Management lands, the so-called public domain. After extensive open-range grazing grew up in the 1870s and 1880s, the Forest Service exerted administrative control over its land in 1906. The public domain lands, however, were not regulated until the Taylor Grazing Act of 1934, when a minimal grazing fee was charged. By any standard, the public grazing lands are in a seriously deteriorated state and have been since a serious

81

drought in the late 1880s. The Dust Bowl years of the 1930s further aggravated their sorry condition.

Ranchers still exercise extraordinary political influence in the BLM through informal connections and a system of advisory boards. As a result, in spite of the chronically poor condition of the federal range, the BLM has relaxed its control over ranchers during the 1980s through cooperative management agreements and other devices. Federal grazing fees remain well below market value. Although comparisons are somewhat difficult, the most recent statistics show that BLM permittees pay an average of $1.35 per animal unit month (AUM) compared to a westwide appraised market value of $6.53 per AUM.

Western ranchers benefit society in many ways—some tangible, others not. They help meet the continuing market demand for beef and lamb. They provide jobs and preserve the awesome space that helps give the West its identity. Although increasingly much is made of corporate control over vast domains of rangeland, ranchers still contribute a way of life that commands our respect, even our awe. In her portrait of ranch life in Wyoming, *The Solace of Open Spaces,* Gretel Ehrlich wrote:

> On a ranch, small ceremonies and private, informal rituals arise. We ride the spring pasture, pick chokecherries in August, skin out a deer in the fall, and in the enactment experience a wordless exhilaration between bouts of plain hard work. Ritual—which could entail a wedding or brushing one's teeth—goes in the direction of life. Through it we reconcile our barbed solitude with the rushing, irreducible conditions of life.

For these and other reasons, Walter Prescott Webb called the ranch cattle industry "perhaps the most unique and distinctive institution that America has produced." Webb wrote that in 1931, before our invention of television or McDonald's, but he made a point that still deserves to be honored.

There are two problems related to the public range that must be solved, and soon. Both involve water. First, ranchers need winter feed for their stock, and they either purchase it or irrigate their own lands. Irrigated agriculture accounts for more than 80 percent of all water use west of the hundredth meridian. Less than half of all western irrigation water is actually consumed by the crops, however, because there are monumental inefficiencies in this use of water, largely due to earthen irrigation ditches and flood irrigation. Defining waste is controversial, because most of the unconsumed water returns to the stream as return flow. And, to be sure, there are ranchers and farmers who have outstandingly efficient systems. In Ivan Doig's *English Creek,* Beth McCaskill said that "Ben English used the water in his namesake creek as a weaver uses wool. With care. With respect." Nonetheless, large amounts of water—23 million acre-feet annually, according to Soil Conservation Service estimates—are irretrievably lost to western river systems through evaporation or consumption by noncrop vegetation. Even the return flow does not reenter the stream in the same condition in which it was diverted; agricultural runoff is likely to be warmer and laden with salts and agricultural chemicals. We have too many stresses on western water quantity and quality to be able to afford these inefficient practices indefinitely.

The second problem, partially traceable to the cattle industry, is even more severe. Uncountable hundreds of millions of tons of soil run off the federal grazing lands every year. Although erosion is more serious, for example, in the Southwest than in Montana and the Dakotas, much of the region is faced with a rampaging erosion that is silting up reservoirs, clouding and warming rivers and streams, and creating sediment loads for downstream consumptive users. Cattle have pounded down the upland grazing areas, driving out many of the native plants and battering the soil and ground cover, destroying their ability to absorb water. Cattle have devastated riparian zones, those green ribbons that are the most productive ecological areas in rangeland systems, growing twenty-five times as much forage as the uplands. Riparian zones are critical to a healthy watershed. Their vegetation and beaver ponds filter and trap sediment, thus building stream banks, regulating stream flow, releasing clean and cool water, and reducing the danger and severity of floods. These spongy areas are the tips of vast groundwater aquifers that store water and provide reliable flows in late summer, when the need for water is the greatest. Riparian zones are also exceptional wildlife habitats. There is no serious disagreement among range scientists about the imperative need to resuscitate those versatile and valuable riparian zones.

An ethic of place, with respect to both the natural resources and to the ranching community, might call for these range issues to be handled in the following manner: to improve water efficiency, ranchers and other irrigators should make improvements, voluntarily or through state government directives, that will substantially alleviate the effects of excessive irrigation diversions. These include lining canals, using sprinklers, and leveling fields. But those who advocate such measures to free up water for new uses must extend an honest respect to the ranching community—virtually an indigenous society in the West. They must insist upon incentive programs so the needed improvement will be within the ranchers' economic capabilities. The water transfer laws ought to be amended so that the ranchers' saved water will be marketable. Low-interest loans and tax incentives should be made available on generous terms. Further, these required reforms directed toward improving efficiency should be phased in over several years, according to local conditions.

Solving the problem of degraded range conditions should proceed by first identifying the real issue. Although the long-standing subsidy for grazing fees is an electric political issue for environmentalists in these Gramm-Rudman days, they must recognize that the subsidy is not the overriding problem. At an estimated $33 million per year, the grazing subsidy is modest compared to other governmental subsidies and is a drop in the bucket of the overall federal budget. Further, low grazing fees are not a substantial and direct cause of poor range conditions. Low grazing fees may not be desirable, but they are not decisive as to the real issue, which is soil and watershed protection.

In addition, there is increasing evidence that poor range conditions are not attributable to the number of cows on the public lands. Allan Savory, an independent ranch consultant who runs Holistic Resource Management out of Santa Fe, has built an impressive case that range quality can actually be improved if the number of cattle is increased. Savory points out that the native grasses in many western watersheds co-evolved with buffalo, and that large ungulates perform numerous functions essential to healthy rangeland. Their hoofs chip up the earth, giving seeds an opportunity to germinate and keeping the soil loose and absorbent. Light grazing of the plants promotes growth, much like pruning does. But, whereas the wild buffalo kept moving across the range, cows need to be managed so that they do not congregate and stay put, especially in riparian zones but also in upland areas. In some severely degraded systems, cows may have to be kept out of riparian zones entirely for several years through the use of exclosures. But, more often, even during the recovery period, cattle can be allowed to graze in all areas of a rangeland system, including riparian zones, so long as they are there at the right time of year for the right length of time. Savory's method is not truly new—it has cousins in rest-rotation and in various BLM experimental projects, most notably Wayne Elmore's work at Camp Creek near Prineville, Oregon—but Savory's personal dynamism and successful academic courses for ranchers and federal employees have personified this reform movement.

But all members of a watershed community should be willing to take chances.

Both environmentalists and ranchers must make major perceived concessions in order for the Savory and Elmore methods to be widely adopted. Environmentalists distrust to their depths the idea of increasing or even maintaining the current number of animal unit months on the public range. Most notably, the Natural Resources Defense Council has spent a decade and a half litigating the level of AUMs—an effort that has drawn public attention to the sorry state of the western range and has required the development of a solid information base through court-ordered National Environmental Protection Act (NEPA) statements. But environmentalists should not insist on stock reductions if, after objective consideration of the Savory and Elmore methods, they are satisfied that existing or increased AUMs can improve the range. Environmentalists ought to support this lessening of the burden on an already stressed ranch economy.

Ranchers also need to bend to accommodate the needs of the region. Like the environmentalists, they should study the Savory method and, if it works, adopt it. Early voluntary readjustment of this kind is the best route. But the BLM must also actively promote progressive range management and see that Savory's innovative approaches, or similar ones, are put in place. In this manner, the real evil in range policy—not the subsidies, not too many cows, but the lack of good range management—can be squarely addressed. Ranchers can no longer simply turn the cattle loose in May and round them up in September; they can achieve a better end product through slightly altered practices.

This approach takes respect on all sides: from the ranchers for the very real damage that has been done to the western range and watercourses and from environmentalists for the very precarious financial situation that ranchers face today. But all members of a watershed community should be willing to take chances. They must assume the risk of departing from old and deeply ingrained stereotypes in order to pursue a course that has every promise of making the watershed a better place from every point of view.

THE BIGHORN BASIN

The Wind River, the major tributary of the Bighorn, heads at the north end of the Wind River Range in Wyoming, flows southeast, and swings north at about the town of Riverton. The river then gains the name Bighorn and moves north into Montana, where it flows mostly within the Crow Indian Reservation before joining the Yellowstone at the small town of Bighorn. It drains about four thousand square miles of land area in Wyoming and a somewhat lesser amount in Montana.

In June 1989, the United States Supreme Court affirmed the decision of the Wyoming Supreme Court in the Bighorn adjudication, which decided water rights in the Wyoming portion of the Bighorn River. This case has been one of the leading pieces of natural resources litigation pending anywhere in the West. It was the first decision handed down by a state court under the newly recognized power of states to adjudicate Indian water rights pursuant to the McCarran Amendment of 1952. The litigation involved all users on the Bighorn River, but focused on the Indians of the Wind River Reservation, which totals about 1.8 million acres on the east side of the Wind River Range. This tribal reservation is an area, it might be noted, larger than Delaware and about two-thirds the size of Connecticut. The litigation, for which the state of Wyoming alone has already appropriated close to $12 million, awarded the tribe reserved rights totaling about 477,000 acre-feet of water, apparently the largest single water right in the basin. The rights of the Crow Tribe on the Montana segment of the river have yet to be resolved.

Traditionally, allocation of interstate waters has been accomplished by interstate compacts or, failing that, by equitable apportionment in the Supreme Court. While the waters of the Bighorn River have been allocated by a compact between the states of Wyoming and Montana, tribal rights were expressly excluded from the compact. Water use is increasingly tight throughout the reaches of the Bighorn, as is the case with most major river systems in the West, especially if coal production in the basin again surges, as it did during the 1970s. As a result, many knowledgeable observers believe that the interstate allocation of the river may need to be reexamined in light of tribal water rights.

An ethic of place would call for a different kind of compact than those used in the past. There is no legal barrier, constitutional or otherwise, to including the Wind River and Crow tribes in the compact negotiations and to providing them with seats on the compact commission, so long as Congress approved the compact, as it must every compact. This would be a full recognition of the tribes' status as sovereign governments within the constitutional system.

There is precedent for such an approach in the sweeping United States-Canada Pacific Salmon Treaty of 1985. Indian tribes participated in those negotiations and were allocated one of four United States seats on the International Pacific Salmon Commission established by the treaty. During the late 1980s, Tim Wapato, a Quinault Indian and executive director of the Columbia River Intertribal Fish Commission, served as the head of the United States delegation to this important international commission.

It is, of course, not for me to suggest the specifics of how these concepts would be employed in the Bighorn Basin. But, whatever the details, the tribal presence on water matters is so important that no basin-wide compact or management plan will be finally workable until tribal governments sit side by side with state governments at the tables where decisions are made. When that occurs, the ethic of place will have been fulfilled in the Bighorn Basin in a historic way.

THE EAGLE RIVER BASIN

The Eagle River Basin in Colorado rises near Tennessee Pass, just north of Leadville. The river flows north and west past Vail and through Eagle before meeting the main Colorado at Dotsero just east of Glenwood Springs. The river is bounded on the northeast by the Gore Range. In the headwaters area lie the Mount of the Holy Cross and the Holy Cross Wilderness.

Two Front Range cities, Aurora and Colorado Springs, want to build the Homestake II Project within the wilderness area. The cities would divert twenty thousand acre-feet of water each year from four creeks in the wilderness and tunnel the water ten miles under the Continental Divide for use in the Eastern Slope cities. The cities would be allowed to divert most of the water in those streams—apparently up to 90 percent—during the spring runoff. The Holy Cross Wilderness Defense Fund and other environmental groups oppose the project because of its destructive effects on wildlife and on the wetlands ecosystem and because of the aesthetic impacts of the diversion dams and intake facilities within this wilderness area.

In February of 1988, the county commissioners of Eagle County, within which the wilderness area is located, denied necessary permits to the cities. The commissioners acted under Colorado's so-called House Bill 1041, which creates areas and activities of state interest that are designated and administered by local governments. It is not finally clear whether water projects are covered under HB 1041—Aurora and Colorado Springs argue that local governments can place no limitations on water diversions—and the decision is being appealed. If HB 1041 cannot be invoked by regions of potential export, there are precious few other protections under existing law in Colorado. The Front Range cities are not covered even by the state's minimal protections afforded to natural basins when water is exported. But one thing is clear: Homestake II is no more popular on the Western Slope than is the Two Forks project, which would also move Western Slope water east to Front Range cities.

Leaving aside environmental concerns, the social component of an ethic of place would require that precise and hard questions be asked about this proposed diversion from the Eagle Valley. Since a major source of water and energy is conservation, could the cities achieve sustained supplies of water from within their own watersheds by adopting improved conservation methods? Even if they adopt rigorous conservation standards, what is the need for the water—projected new development many years hence? And if that is the need, why exactly is it that such a need should stunt the fulfillment of other communities in another watershed? The ethic requires us to ask even other questions, which must trouble every westerner. What will it finally take to wean us from a pace of development that cannot be acceptably maintained at the rate it has proceeded since World War II? What sort of places will there be in the West if we allow that pace to continue? Are we willing to leave it to our bright-eyed children and grandchildren to live with the stark consequences of the answers?

THE RIO CHAMA VALLEY

The Rio Chama arises in Colorado's San Juan Mountains, but almost all of its run is in New Mexico. It enters the main stem of the Rio Grande near Espanola. Part of the Jicarilla Apache Reservation occupies some of the high country along the Continental Divide in the northwest part of the basin, and numbers of Anglos live along the Rio Chama, but from the top to the bottom of the valley the overwhelming presence is of Hispanic people and their ranching and farming communities.

One of the most intriguing recent judicial decisions in western water law is a 1985 trial court ruling by District Judge Art Encinias, sitting in Rio Arriba County in the Rio Chama Valley. The state engineer had granted an application to change the diversion point, purpose, and place of use of surface water rights. The existing use was for irrigation, and the purpose of the proposed changes was to provide water for a ski resort and guest ranch. There was no transfer out of the basin, so area of origin statutes did not come into play. The rarely invoked New Mexico public interest statute provides that new appropriations may be disapproved by the state engineer if "approval thereof would be contrary to the public interest." The statutes relating to changes of existing appropriations, however, contain no such language. Nevertheless, the trial judge set aside the administrative action because in his view it was contrary to the local

What will it finally take to wean us from a pace of development that cannot be acceptably maintained at the rate it has proceeded at since World War II?

public interest. In a spirit reminiscent of *The Milagro Beanfield War,* John Nichols's novel (and now movie) about water, which cannot be called fiction, Judge Encinias wrote this:

> Northern New Mexicans possess a fierce pride over their history, traditions and culture. This region of northern New Mexico and its living culture are recognized at the state and federal levels as possessing significant cultural value, not measurable in dollars and cents. The deep-felt and tradition bound ties of northern New Mexico families to the land and water are central to the maintenance of that culture. . . .
>
> I am persuaded that to transfer water rights, devoted for more than a century to agricultural purposes, in order to construct a playground for those who can pay is a poor trade, indeed. I find that the proposed transfer of water rights is clearly contrary to the public interest and, on that separate basis, the Application should be denied.

Judge Encinias may have reached the wrong legal result. Indeed, his ruling was later reversed by the New Mexico Supreme Court on narrow grounds. But whether or not this particular legal point stands up, I think there is something quintessential in the reasoning, a melding of tradition, economics, and outrage that may ultimately find a secure place in the law of New Mexico and many another state. This is because Judge Encinias knew his place, the valley of the Rio Chama. He knew the land and the economy. He knew the long drama of his people, for he wrote from the same stolid stucco courthouse in Tierra Amarilla that Reies Tijerina and his men had besieged just a generation earlier, in 1967, in their quest to enforce the old Mexican and Spanish land and water grants supposedly protected by the United States in the Treaty of Guadalupe Hidalgo.

Cultural considerations play a much greater role in law than we commonly realize. In New Mexico, for example, the state provides tax credits for preservation of cultural property; has an extensive statutory procedure for designating cultural properties; has strong statutory provisions for bilingual, multicultural education; promotes Indian arts and crafts by statute; and recognizes Indian pueblos.

Western water law assumes a priori that cultural factors have no place in allocating water, but most sensible people not steeped in prior appropriation would think that an old culture's tie to the land must figure in the allocation equation as a matter of course. One can easily imagine that if some sage outside observer—say a de Tocqueville of the late twentieth century—came through the Rio Chama Valley, spent some time there, and read Judge Encinias's opinion, such a visitor would say, "Of course, of course"—because a sense of place is a powerful thing and ought to be reflected in a people's laws.

WATER FOR URBAN USES

Themes of water policy and law run throughout this essay, as they do throughout life in the American West, and it is worthwhile to note briefly that there are several instances—important ones—in which our approach toward water has begun to broaden and to incorporate the environmental, cultural, and community objectives that are required by an ethic of place.

These developments are evidenced in one of the most intransigent of all western policy issues, the provision of water to growing urban areas. Historically, urban water issues have been exemplified by Los Angeles's turn-of-the-century raid—it was nothing short of that—of the water, economy, and society of Owens Valley, 225 miles to the north on the other side of the Sierra Nevada.

The sequel to the Owens Valley saga, however, is in the process of taking a very different turn. In the 1940s, Los Angeles reached still further north to divert from four of the five creeks feeding Mono Lake. When the lake level dropped dramatically, threatening the rich wildlife population there, the Audubon Society and local citizens' organizations sued. Their position, based on the public trust doctrine, was sustained in a 1983 California Supreme Court decision. The ruling on Mono Lake is a leading acknowledgment of the demands of westerners that instream flows be recognized as part of a sensible body of water law. The court decision left many issues still remaining to be negotiated at Mono Lake. Today, the Los Angeles Department of Water and Power, environmental organizations, and local interest groups are close to a settlement that will protect the lake, allow Los Angeles to continue diverting a lesser but substantial amount of water, and respect the right of communities on the eastern side of the Sierra to have a considerable say over the use of their area's water.

Negotiations between rural and urban interests have born fruit elsewhere. In December 1989, the Imperial Irrigation District (IID) and the Municipal Water District (MWD), serving metropolitan Southern California, reached an accord. The agreement calls for MWD to fund an extensive water conservation program at IID; the saved water, about 100,000 acre-feet per year, will be used by MWD.

Another, less well-known, example arose in the early 1980s, when Los Angeles first attempted to obtain water for the Intermountain Power Project (IPP) in western Utah by purchasing water rights at bargain-basement rates directly from individual farmers in the Sevier River watershed. Instead, the farmers banded together and ultimately negotiated a settlement that based all sales of water on Los Angeles values (about $1,750/acre-foot) rather than Utah prices (between $3 and $500/acre-foot); provided for a purchase of less water than originally contemplated by Los Angeles, so that as much land as possible could remain in agricultural production; and required the lease-back of purchased water to farmers if the power plant did not require as much water as planned. Today, very little land in the Sevier Valley has gone out of farming: Los Angeles downscaled IPP and farmers spent some of the proceeds from the water sales for water conservation measures so that farmland could keep operating with less water. As a general matter, the infusion of capital from the water rights purchases and the power plant has boosted the local economy. As Mike Clinton, the widely respected former U.S. Department of Interior official, has said of Delta, Utah, the nearest town to IPP, "The economy is again robust. No longer are storefronts boarded up, and the young people don't have to move to the cities to find jobs. The community has a new lease on life."

These are not simple matters. Western water issues seldom are. The spirit of arms-length negotiations—of respect—evident at Mono Lake, Imperial, and IPP may not prove to be the wave of the future. But, for the moment, these events sound hopeful notes that deserve our best listening.

One implicit theme in the ethic of place is that we westerners fail to aspire high enough. We fail to ask the hard but right questions. How great a society can we build? Should greatness be denied to us because our sophistication is of a different kind than Paris of the 1920s or ancient Rome or Athens? Are we somehow disqualified from greatness because we tend to build our philosophies around deep back canyons and the sweep of high plains vistas? Is the quality of our personal relationships less because we draw our sustenance, not from rapid-fire intellectual head banging, but from putting brakes on things, from toeing at the ground or pausing at the pass to look back over where we have been?

Another undercurrent involves romanticism. Although the ethic of place is solidly positioned on economics, ecology, several physical sciences, law, and the psychology of interpersonal relationships, we can also find a streak of what can be fairly called romanticism. But I refuse to allow that to be a conversation stopper. Romanticism—or, put somewhat differently, beauty, imagination, cultural conservatism, and a love of history—is as real as youth, the market, the environment, or art. All are part of the landscape of the mind and we deny something fundamental in ourselves if we deny the tangible existence of any of them.

The single greatest ally of those who would wreck the West is the idea that the West is homogeneous. If there is nothing special and distinctive about a silver current twining down a back canyon; or the hard-caked ruts that you can see today and that were, really were, made by the wagons of the women and men who came over the Oregon Trail; or a wolf or an eagle; or a rancher putting up fence; or a tribal judge trying to blend the old and the new, and many different cuts of conscience, when he or she rules on whether the Navajo child should remain with her white adoptive parents or be awarded to a Navajo family; or yet another aspen grove on yet another forty-five-degree canyon wall; or an old Hispanic mayordomo going out to clean out the mother ditch—if none of those things is special, then we might as well do away with them, each of them.

We are taught by sophisticated people that regionalism is passé. Let us not participate in that and let us not permit our children to participate in it. Let us take the emotional and intellectual chance of saying that this is not the leftover sector of our nation; that, rather, this is the true soul of the country, the place that cries out loudest to the human spirit; that this place is exalted, that it is sacred. Use that word, sacred; and whatever kind of ethic it is, use the word ethic, because the word properly connotes high things.

Last, let us be sure to say these things to all of the people, for the contentiousness really can wane when we realize, and act upon, our common melded past and future. For, as Wallace Stegner has written in *The Sound of Mountain Water,* when the West "finally learns that cooperation, not rugged individualism, is the pattern that most characterizes and preserves it, then it will have achieved itself and outlived its origins. Then it has a chance to create a society to match its scenery."

Essay excerpted from *The Eagle Bird Has Landed: Searching for an Ethic of Place.* Reprinted with permission of the publisher, Howe Brothers.

Paintbrush. Albion Basin, Utah. Photo © Tom Till.

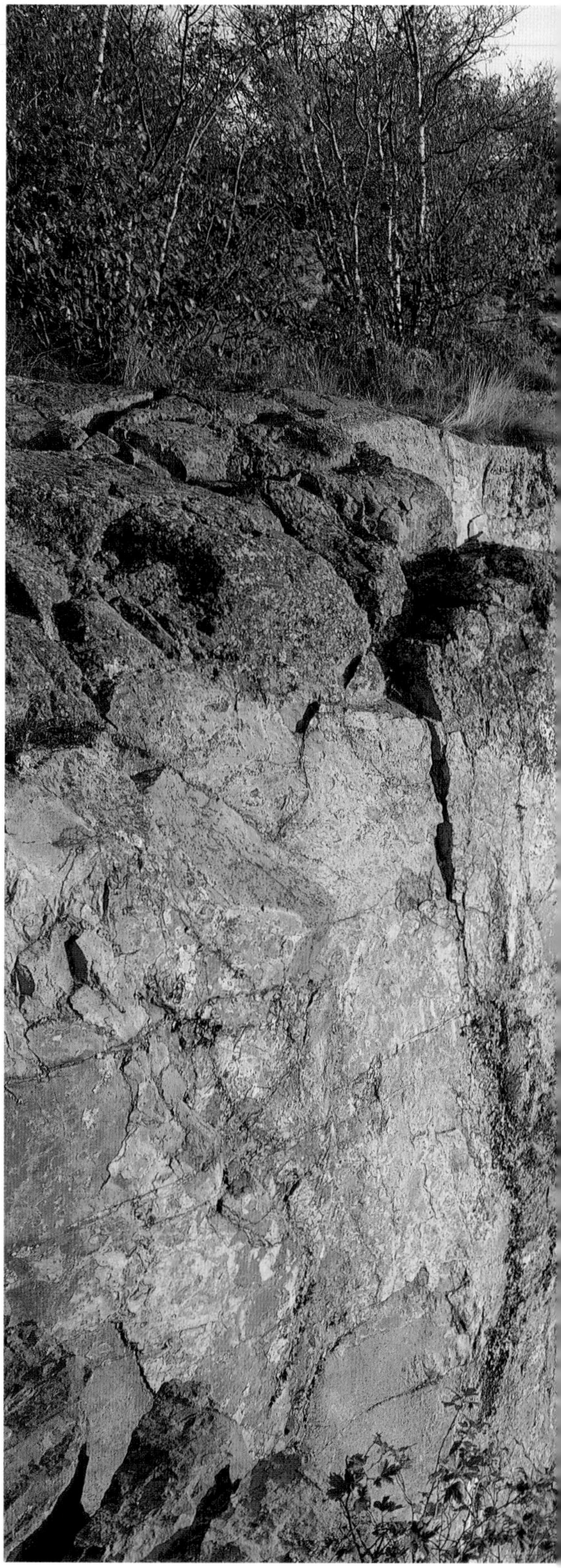

Lake Superior, Minnesota.
Photo © Tom Till

Poker Jim Ridge above Warner Lakes Valley, Oregon. Photo © George Wuerthner.

Coast north of Brookings, Samuel Boardman State Park, Oregon. Photo © George Wuerthner.

Tufa formations, Pyramid Lake Reservation, Nevada. Photo © Tom Till.

Mount Ranier National Park, Washington. Photo © George Wuerthner.

Hoh Rainforest, Olympic National Park, Washington. Photo © Tom Till.

Fall leaves at St. Croix River State Park, Minnesota. Photo © Tom Till.

RETHINKING DEVELOPMENT AND THE WESTERN ENVIRONMENT
John M. Volkman

In Salt Lake City, where I grew up, rain smells like the dust that the raindrops kick up. Irrigation is the only reason there are trees, and it is easy to understand why people fight over water. Watching Salt Lake City expand toward the Oquirrh Mountains, the question in my mind was how the valley was going to find water to sustain that kind of growth. It seemed to me that at some point we would run out of extra water.

In some kinds of poker, there is a moment when bluffs are called, everyone has to think carefully about how much money to bet, and "hole cards," which have not yet been revealed to other players, are evaluated seriously. Somewhere, there was a hole card in the hand the valley had been dealt, and some day, it seemed to me, the valley would find that its hole card was too low.

What bothered me about hole cards was not that they might be there, but that there was so little serious discussion about what they might look like and how they might be played. Were we really living in a fool's paradise? Surely not; the valley had been settled by people who had first-hand experience with aridity. Perhaps they had some instinctive sense of the hydrologic limits of the place, and this was passed down from generation to generation. But as I grew older, I abandoned this belief, and I took it for granted that people were thinking about things other than hole cards. My concern that the valley's development might not be sustainable in the long run has never gone away.

When I moved to Oregon, my shoes got soggy on the way to work, and I lost some of this concern. Western Oregon still seems to me to be

East of Mullen, Hooker County, Nebraska. Photo © Jon Farrar.

hopelessly wet. Moss grows on the roof, and if I don't clean out rain gutters, plants will sprout in them. The rain grows big trees and impenetrable thickets. It is hard not to take the Northwest's water and forests for granted.

I have come to understand, however, that there are never enough resources, whether they are water or something else, and hole cards lurk even in the lushest places. Soggy shoes and all, I am knee-deep in issues that stem from conflicts over water. I work with the legacy of a conflict between river-based resources: the Columbia River's hydropower dams and the salmon and steelhead runs that migrate throughout the river system. If it is unfortunate that these resources are involved in collisions and near-collisions; at least these collisions have pushed the Northwest beyond the point of ignoring hole cards. What is more hopeful is that a system has emerged from these collisions in which an entire region can examine resource conflicts openly, and try to develop common understandings of how to resolve them.

Fifty years from now, these collisions may look like minor bumps and nudges, and the Northwest's system for adjusting disputes may be a quaint antique, but for now it is worth examining in some detail. The West has many collisions in its future, and few ways of resolving them that take long-term interests into account.

New development in the West is increasingly constrained by the accumulated effects of past development, and developers are having to foot the bill for solving problems rooted in the past. Western tourism is big business, an important hedge against traditional industry busts, and its future depends on the preservation of unspoiled land. Yet, tourism is not a universal answer. In areas where tourism offers little hope, depressed economies may undermine environmental protection.

A vigorous international debate is developing over what is called "sustainable development"—the notion, as a member of the World Commission on Environment and Development put it, that "it is only by changing the nature and the dynamics of [the] economic process that we will be able to grow in ways that will permit us to continue that growth, and to do so on a basis that will not undermine the quality of human life."

The West, like it or not, will play a role in that debate. All of these conflicting pressures—western, national, and international hole cards—will have to be balanced in some fashion. The Northwest's experience in juggling the developmental interests represented by electric power and the environmental values represented by salmon, is a case study in the search for this balance, and it offers lessons for other parts of the West.

I will talk about sustainable development, not in the abstract, but by discussing the problem of making it a workable idea. I concentrate on the role of government because so much of the West is either owned or regulated by government—primarily the federal government, which owns about half the West's land. Federal agencies charged with managing these resources are likely to be the focus in conflicts over western natural resources, which include national parks, forests, grazing land, Indian reservations, and their associated resources. If the objective is to find economic activity that is environmentally sustainable, these agencies represent key leverage points.

To set the stage for this discussion, I will describe some of the obstacles that stand in the way of a clear view of the economic and environmental issues posed by western resource conflicts. Next, I will describe the Northwest's experience in attempting to work through these obstacles, and suggest some lessons for other areas of the West.

OBSTACLES TO SUSTAINABLE WESTERN DEVELOPMENT POLICY

Try to explain to a seven year-old how we decide what resources we will develop in the West, and how we go about accounting for environmental concerns. I confess I haven't yet attempted it, but I intend to, and this is a warm-up. The broad concept of sustainable development offers a little help, because it conveys the idea that development must be able to sustain itself over the long term. But it is such a general concept that it makes resource choices sound too easy; why don't we just do it, the seven-year-old will say. It sounds easy. To convey the problem, the obstacles have to be understood. I group these obstacles under three headings: (1) fragmentation; (2) problems in valuing rivers, animals, and other natural resources in dollars; and (3) uncertainty.

Fragmentation. Natural resource agencies tend to be organized along the lines of particular resources—rangeland agencies, forest agencies, energy agencies, water agencies, fish and wildlife agencies, and so forth. The fragmentation created by this assortment of jurisdictions can be complex enough in a single state. When a resource transcends state boundaries, the complications can be spectacular. At last count, an upriver salmon in the Columbia River system could pass through as many as seventeen jurisdictions with some degree of authority to manage salmon harvest, and the number would be higher if land and water use agencies with jurisdiction over salmon habitat were included. Each entity has different responsibilities, concerns, and expertise, and each must be coordinated to meet the needs of the resource and its users. Federal agencies with broad but not comprehensive authorities look at western resources through their own prisms, which may reflect western realities but also must respond to pressures in Washington, D.C. State agencies representing a variety of developmentally or environmentally oriented interests retain some prerogatives and battle with federal agencies over others. Environmentalists and tribes go to federal court, where agency determinations can be held up to penetrating inquiry. Checks and balances run riot, developers expend time and money satisfying disparate requirements, and agency boundaries become obstacles to coherent vision. Perhaps this system works, in some sense, as checks and balances can work. But comprehensive vision and long-term, sustainable patterns of growth are likely to fall between the cracks.

Finding a cure for this fragmentation is not a trivial matter, however. Limitations in agency jurisdictions are rooted in law and politics. Mission-oriented agencies like the Army Corps of Engineers have powerful constituencies. Resistance to the federal agencies is often deeply rooted, as the Sagebrush Rebellion of recent years reminds us. And, of course, resistance to powerful government agencies is part of America's heritage. The Framers of the Constitution had seen the excesses of which government is capable, and they wrote a constitution that is, in important respects, an anti-government instrument. This raises a dilemma in the debate over sustainable development. Government administration capable of charting a strategic course for western resource management implies centralized administration; but centralized agencies are likely to run up against the country's deep mistrust of government power.

Problems in valuing natural resources in dollars. Why can't we put a dollar value on the positive and negative impacts of development, add and subtract them, and choose the alternative with the most value? In theory, economic analysis can do this, putting dollar values on environmental and economic costs and benefits, providing an objective basis for decision making, and correcting myopia in government determinations.

The reality, however, falls short. Historically, development decisions were short-term, profit-oriented decisions. Environmental costs were not often counted, either because they were hard to see, or because they were not seen as real costs. In the jargon of economists, environmental costs are "externalities" that for one reason or another are not included in the cost of producing goods.

The problem of externalities has long plagued management of public resources, and natural resource commentators have created colorful metaphors to convey what externalities are. Garrett Hardin's "tragedy of the commons" describes the situation in which no one has an incentive to conserve a common resource because no one is required to pay the full cost of exploitation. William Ruckelshaus describes resources as capital: "In violation of the core principle of capitalism, we often refuse to treat environmental resources as capital. We spend them as income and are as befuddled as any profligate heir when our checks start to bounce." In my mind, I see a story from my family's history in the California gold rush. In 1875, my great-great-grandmother made a trip to the family's former home, a ranch called Garden Valley. When she was a child in the 1850s, Garden Valley had been "beautifully located between high mountains, about two miles long and three fourths of a mile wide from foothill to foothill, with a stream of clear, rushing water running through it." In 1875,

Garden Valley had been covered to a depth of almost fifty feet with debris washed down Willow Creek from the different mining camps. Mother and I walked over from Foster's Bar and looked down from a hill on our old home, where we had spent such happy years.

Comprehensive vision and long-term, sustainable patterns of growth are likely to fall between cracks.

109

The house was covered, the orchard, the stable, Mother's wonderful milk-house—everything. It was nothing but a great valley of sand and yellow clay.

Garden Valley was an externality, buried under the runoff from hydraulic mining from Sierra Nevada gold fields.

Costs that could be externalized in the nineteenth century are no longer so casually tolerated. As a consultant to the Denver Water Board summed up the predicament of Two Forks Dam, a stalled water development near Denver, "We're no longer living on the frontier. You can't do much without affecting your neighbor. And your neighbor has recourse."

Laws and agency practices have taken account of some externalities. In building coal plants, for example, developers must now count the cost of scrubbers and other pollution controls required by law. Where government agencies are themselves the developers, the agencies conduct elaborate environmental impact statements, replete with cost-benefit analyses intended to identify economic and environmental costs, including externalities, and to identify suitable environmental mitigation.

This trend is not altogether welcomed by developers or environmentalists. To developers, ignoring externalities lowers production costs, and environmental laws requiring these costs to be paid are unwelcome. To environmentalists, these remedies do not go far enough. Coal scrubbers remove some pollutants but not others, and the pollutants that are removed may only be flushed into the water, where they are treated, aerated, and returned to the air. Externalities remain, and each session of Congress sees new efforts to "close the loop" in environmental regulation, fought by industries seeking to keep development costs low.

Cost-benefit analyses used by government agencies fare little better. A cost-benefit analysis may identify some environmental costs, but to environmentalists, the analysis may appear wildly misleading. As C. L. Rawlins, a writer for *High Country News* put it, "A cost-benefit analysis reduces the world from its bright, wet, salty, rocky, sandy, snow-covered, floral, shaggy grace to columns of digits that don't have even the virtue of being real money; economists call them projections rather than fantasies; they should call them spells.''

Comparing economic and environmental values in economic terms puts environmental values at a disadvantage. We presume development is beneficial because we can do a reasonably good job of quantifying economic benefits. Yet environmental externalities persist because we can find few tools—and even those are imperfect—for measuring environmental values, and we are reluctant to pay for things we cannot measure.

Uncertainty. The agencies' ability to compare economic and environmental values is complicated by uncertainty in demand for resources. The problem was illustrated by the energy boom of the 1970s and '80s. In the 1970s, the prediction was for steady growth in energy demand. An ambitious energy development program created a boom in the several states that reverberated throughout western economies. Many previously untouched parts of the West became sites for aggressive mineral exploration. When demand for power fell off in the early 1980s, parts of the West had energy surpluses to go along with an economic bust. The resources that were consumed by the boom seem, from the vantage point of the bust, to have been needlessly used up. Once-quiet communities became boom towns and many just in time for the bust.

Something similar happened in the Pacific Northwest. With forecasts of continued economic growth, the region's electric utilities began a massive nuclear construction campaign. Billions of dollars in bonds were marketed on Wall Street, and construction was begun on five nuclear plants, with four more on the drawing boards. Ten years into the effort, the program turned sour, plagued by cost overruns, lengthening construction schedules, and concern over waste disposal. When the program collapsed in the early 1980s, investors lost billions of dollars, and wholesale federal electric rates increased fivefold. The predicted energy deficit, moreover, turned out to be a surplus. Developers had relied on forecasts—of energy demand, construction costs, and other variables—and the results were disastrous. Having been badly burned, many utilities today are reluctant to take risks on new energy development.

One response to these uncertainties is to strive for better predictions, but this only creates an illusion of certainty. The old electric utility industry saying—''it's hard to predict anything, especially the future''— has more truth to it than humor. Forecasts are valuable because they help decision makers come to grips with what may face them, not just because they predict the future. Assumptions underlying forecasts should be challenged, analytical models criticized, and alternative projections made. These exercises improve policy debates, which often call for judgments based on compromise and consensus in any event. Possibilities, generalities, and rough numbers may be more important than fine detail. Over-meticulous forecasting can be an unproductive use of effort, or worse, can narrow options, limit debate, foreclose compromise, and lead to costly mistakes.

Uncertainty requires an evaluation of risks and benefits, not techniques for assuming uncertainty away.

Uncertainty frustrates environmentalists in other ways. To take a prominent example, currently there is widespread concern over the prospect of global warming. Experts agree that some warming will occur, and environmentalists urge government to take bold action. Some experts, however, counsel caution—the assumptions on which computer model projections are based are crude, and knowledge of the world climate is too scant to tell us how much warming will occur, or where. In this view, policy makers should wait for better models and forecasts before taking action. Similar arguments arise in debates over acid rain, air and water pollution, and countless other environmental issues. These uncertainties result in inaction, rather than efforts to control the risk of irreparable environmental losses.

Environmentalists also face risks created by uncertainty in mitigation programs. Environmental mitigation attempts to restore damaged natural environments. In fact, however, natural environments are complex and poorly understood, and mitigation programs can only restore a simpler, less resilient environment than was lost. Foresters replacing an indigenous forest with new, fast-growing species of trees create a homogenous forest that cannot regain the unique biological niche the natural forest had carved for itself. Homogenized hatchery salmon lack the mettle that enable wild salmon to migrate far into the interior reaches of the West. On occasion, environmental mitigation programs beat the odds and surpass our expectations, but more often they fail, sometimes disastrously, and at a cost that can only be guessed.

These factors—government fragmentation, limitations in economic analysis, and economic and environmental uncertainty—begin to explain why it is hard to "just do" sustainable development in the West. Next I will describe the Northwest program, as it responds to each obstacle.

THE NORTHWEST POWER PLANNING COUNCIL

In the late 1970s, the Northwest was faced with what appeared to be two crises rushing headlong toward collision. The first was a crisis over electric power supply, which seemed to require large new sources of power. The second was a sharp decline in salmon runs due to the effects of power dams. At a time when the region's power supply was under great strain, operation of the dams might have to be curtailed to permit the recovery of a treasured resource, the Columbia River's salmon runs.

Each of these crises brought out divisions that were less apparent in palmier times. The Northwest has always been a high energy user because of the cheap, relatively abundant power available from the federal dams on the Columbia River. When the region ran out of new hydropower capacity from the river, however, utilities without access to cheap federal power were prepared to fight those who had access. Indian tribes were locked in litigation with state fish and wildlife agencies over the right to harvest the remnant salmon. Hydropower developers offended a broad range of interests, aggressively pushing small dams that large utilities were required by law to subsidize, and invading salmon spawning grounds.

Government fragmentation that in other times was merely inconvenient became a significant problem. Federal dams, power lines, and other facilities were central to the region's energy system, but federal agency jurisdictions overlapped and competed; long-simmering tensions between public and private utilities were imbedded in government power agencies; no single agency could implement a coherent energy strategy for the region. Fishery management was divided among states, federal fishery agencies, and Indian tribes, who had spent years fighting each other. None of the parties had a clear way to make power dams remedy their

Uncertainty requires an evaluation of risks and benefits, not techniques for assuming uncertainty away.

113

impacts on fish and wildlife. With added authorization from Congress, these problems could be addressed by a single federal agency. However, neither the states nor the region's utilities wanted to give a federal agency additional, unfettered authority over the region's power system.

The economic uncertainties facing the region were huge. When in the 1970s the region's utilities had settled on nuclear power and coal as their primary sources for new electricity, energy demand had been projected to grow steadily. After a ten-year, multi-billion-dollar investment in nuclear plants, however, the region was left with a collection of partially built plants, an oversupply of electricity, and a huge debt. Future demand was uncertain, and few were anxious to assume new risks without some way of spreading the risks more broadly.

Fish and wildlife managers were unsure how to counteract the effects of the dams, and had scant power to make the attempt. Hatchery programs designed to mitigate the impacts of the dams had weakened wild fish stocks, spread disease, and undermined the diversity of the Columbia River runs. New technologies intended to pass juvenile fish safely past dams had in some cases succeeded and in some cases failed, and large parts of the river had been blocked from salmon migration altogether. Worse, it was hard to say what would work, or why. Data were sparse, measurements inexact, and there was no body of biological theory pointing to clear solutions. Solutions such as improved river flows or putting habitat off-limits to development were resisted by development agencies and utilities because of their costs.

To fish and wildlife interests, it was plain that the power system had been subsidized by fish and wildlife, which had not been accounted for in deciding to build the power dams. To environmentalists, coal and nuclear power appeared to have become the region's primary sources of new electricity without fully weighing their environmental costs. An alternative to coal and nuclear power plants—energy conservation—hadn't been given serious consideration. From the vantage point of fish and wildlife agencies, Indian tribes, and environmentalists, federal development agencies had carefully considered the economic benefits of development, but had been less careful when it came to environmental costs.

The situation augured long-term paralysis, which neither the power system nor fish and wildlife interests could afford. Instead of paralysis, however, the Northwest reacted with an unusual package of institutional reforms and policy departures, which Congress passed in the Northwest Power Act of 1980.

OVERCOMING FRAGMENTATION

To reduce the institutional and geographic balkanization that made it so difficult for the region to carry out a coherent energy strategy, Congress gave additional authority to the the Bonneville Power Administration, which owns and operates the regional power grid, to address power needs and the fish and wildlife problems that had been caused by the federal power system. Bonneville's exercise of this authority, however, would be guided by power and fish and wildlife plans developed through a state-based entity, the Northwest Power Planning Council, composed of gubernatorial appointees from the four Northwest states. The council would be a forum in which the full range of interested parties could work through policy questions. Bonneville would be an accessible implementing agency, incorporating the region's decisions into federal processes and, importantly, using a portion of its $3 billion annual revenues to fund power and fish and wildlife initiatives identified in the council's plans. Both the Northwest Council and Bonneville were directed to actively encourage broad participation in their processes.

These arrangements addressed the problem of government fragmentation and the federal-state tensions that pervade western resource management, but without taking on either problem frontally. The federal agencies, with their own jurisdictions and authorities, would remain, but with a new responsibility to help implement the council's plans. State agencies and Indian tribes would not be bound by the council's plans, but were drawn into the arrangement by incentives. Because the council's plan would guide federal investments and activities, if state agencies and tribes could influence the council, they stood to gain. By requiring broad public participation in the council's processes, Congress injected new political forces into the policy process, creating public expectations that resource determinations reached in a comprehensive regional debate would be respected. Altogether, the Northwest process attempted to provide a framework in which resource policy issues could be addressed comprehensively by the council, and implemented without attempting to blast existing agencies loose from entrenched jurisdictions.

Managing uncertainty in power planning. To plan for the region's long-term power supply, the Northwest Council had to take a fresh look at the uncertainties facing the region's power system. With the region still smarting from the disastrously mistaken forecasts of the 1970s, the council expressly recognized that unpredictability had to be a starting point in analyzing energy needs. A range of demand forecasts was prepared, and instead of debating which forecast was the most likely, the council asked what mix of energy resources could meet regional demand wherever it materialized within the range.

To meet demand, Congress had established a priority of resources in which energy conservation—efficient buildings, factories, farms, appliances, lights, generators, and the like—would be the region's preferred resource. Other cost-effective resources, such as hydropower, cogeneration, and others, would follow in order of priority. Conservation and improved energy efficiency were the resources preferred by Congress and the region for two principal reasons: in many cases they are the cheapest alternative, and they are environmentally benign compared to other energy resources.

The other reason to prefer energy conservation and efficiency is that they help reduce risk. Unlike large power plants, energy conservation could be quickly installed in small, inexpensive increments. Once a market for conservation is established, enormous investments should not be required years in advance of operation. Best of all, energy needs can be met if and when demand grows. If energy demand turns out to be lower than expected, no unneeded power plants will have been built, and efficiency improvement programs can be slowed. As the Northwest Council looked at the range of energy alternatives available to the region in the early 1980s, it appeared that improved energy efficiencies could postpone the need for new power plants for at least a decade, and probably well into the next century. If true, this would substantially lessen the uncertainties facing the region.

Learning to put a value on conserving resources. Before the Northwest Council could count on energy efficiencies to satisfy future demand, it had to be satisfied that efficiencies were cost-effective. Congress had defined cost-effective to mean resources that are reliable, available, and whose economic and environmental costs are lowest compared to the alternatives. By this definition, energy efficiency and conservation became ways to more fully account for environmental values. Efficiency and conservation would forestall the need to develop resources—to build a dam or a coal plant—and thereby help minimize environmental impacts.

For these reasons, calculating the cost of conservation and energy efficiency improvements became a matter of particular importance, and Congress directed the council to develop a fairer economic scale on which to compare energy efficiency with traditional energy development. The approach, now called "least-cost planning," required the council to identify all the quantifiable environmental costs and benefits of a full range of reliable and available energy alternatives. Next, energy efficiency measures would be assigned a 10-percent credit to reflect their unquantifiable environmental advantages. The resulting calculations would lead to a stack of energy alternatives called a "resource portfolio," with the least costly resources placed first in the stack, and the most costly resources placed last. The resources in the portfolio could be drawn on to meet energy demands as they materialize.

Recognizing that the balance between economic and environmental factors could not be struck on the basis of mathematics alone, the council elaborated on these instructions. Numerical calculations notwithstanding, some resources may be placed higher or lower in the resource stack based on their reliability, availability, or their unquantifiable environmental characteristics. Such matters could be debated as policy questions, for which cost-effectiveness calculations provide a framework. After debate with interested parties in the region, the council could identify the least costly and most environmentally benign combination of developments to meet the region's needs.

To date, this approach has served the region in an era of energy surplus, a condition that defied the expectations on which the Northwest Power Act was based. No new generating plants were built in the 1980s, in large part because of the energy surplus. With the council pressing for a long-term view of energy needs, however, substantial investments in energy conservation were made. As the 1990s begin and the region's energy surplus is disappearing, this energy conservation investment is estimated to have saved the Northwest nearly a billion and a half dollars compared with the cost of the same amount of power from coal plants, and this figure does not account fully for savings in cleaner air, reduced pressure on other natural resources, and the like. The acid test of the region's commitment to least-cost planning is still coming, as energy needs grow more demanding. In that test, the region will learn how well least-cost planning accounts for environmental costs. At this point, it appears to provide a framework in which environmental and economic questions can be addressed on a more equal footing, and helps focus on the need to explore conservation as doggedly as other resources are explored.

Managing uncertainty in fish and wildlife mitigation. The Northwest Council has missions in two seemingly opposite directions. It aims not just to expand the region's energy options, but to enhance fish and wildlife populations affected by the power dams. This meant that protecting fish and wildlife from the effects of new power development would not be enough; the council had to find ways to address the effects of past development. An unprecedented effort in biological restoration was called for.

When it came to new dams, there were compelling reasons for the council to take a conservative approach to development. From a power perspective, new power dams in prime fish and wildlife habitat would impose high costs and high risks on the region. The cost of mitigation would be high, and the risk that proposed developments would fail to materialize would be increased because of environmental opposition. It would pay to avoid pitched battles between fish and wildlife advocates and developers. From a fish and wildlife perspective, new power dams posed unmistakable risks. Some habitat would be lost to any new development, and the gamble, which few fish and wildlife advocates would willingly take, was that the developer could counteract the loss with a mitigation program. Virtually every mitigation tool except habitat protection involved a significant risk of failure. With the council's responsibility to enhance fish and wildlife populations, prime fish and wildlife habitat was at a premium.

Accordingly, under the aegis of the council and the Bonneville Power Administration, teams of experts and interested parties took on the task of identifying prime fish and wildlife habitat to be protected from new hydropower development. After two years of collecting and evaluating data on fish and wildlife habitat in the region's river corridors, and a year of public review and debate, the council and Bonneville adopted measures to protect some 44,000 stream miles—about 15 percent of the region's river miles—from new hydropower projects. These so-called protected areas are intended to guide the Federal Energy Regulatory Commission in its dam-licensing processes, and Bonneville in its transmission of power outside the region.

The more obdurate and expensive problem was to counteract the effects of the existing hydropower dams. The council began by recognizing that the task was largely unprecedented, and the techniques of the effort were obscure. There were no scientific signposts pointing to successful mitigation; data on key biological variables were spotty; the record of past mitigation was mixed at best; and the economic and biological stakes were high. Yet, because of the critical status of the salmon runs, the council could not delay while mitigation alternatives were tested further. The Northwest Power Act created a special role for the region's fish and wildlife agencies and Indian tribes, and the council relied heavily on their judgment. The act also required the council to proceed on the basis of the "best available scientific knowledge," however, and the council had to push for better understanding.

In response, Professor Kai Lee, who served on the council from 1983 through 1987, suggested that if the effects of mitigation could not be predicted, the council should proceed by using mitigation measures to explore key uncertainties. This approach, developed in natural resource management over the last decade, was termed "adaptive management." It asserted that of course the consequences of mitigation actions would be uncertain; but if mitigation efforts were structured as experiments, the council could learn from success or failure. This signaled a departure from traditional mitigation in two respects. First, adaptive management

In short, adaptive management requires a social and political process, not just a scientific method.

puts a high value on mitigation activities that are likely to illuminate key uncertainties, not just on activities that are supported by intuition or precedent. Risk—financial and biological—could be accepted in exchange for better knowledge. Second, recognizing that experimenting with public resources raises political questions, adaptive management requires a truly collaborative mitigation process. Critical hypotheses have to be identified; data must be compiled and reviewed by interested parties; computer models may be jointly developed; experimental designs and monitoring and evaluation mechanisms have to be debated. There are political and financial limits to this kind of experimentation, and these must be openly confronted. In short, adaptive management requires a social and political process, not just a scientific method.

From an economic point of view, fish and wildlife mitigation posed different questions than were involved in energy planning. Under the Northwest Power Act, power generation would pay the full cost of producing power, including fish and wildlife costs; biological considerations would drive the region's fish and wildlife program. However, Congress cautioned that economic limits were not irrelevant—fish and wildlife mitigation should not ''unreasonably'' burden the power system, or undermine the system's ability to meet regional power needs. With this set of mixed signals, Congress created a weak economic constraint.

The weak economic constraint has its own advantages and disadvantages. The fish and wildlife program has been better funded than any mitigation effort that preceded it. Approximately $30–35 million in out-of-pocket expenditures were spent annually on fish and wildlife mitigation in recent years. Another $60–75 million in power revenues are foregone in an average year, to provide water flows and dam spills for salmon. The problem, however, is illustrated by these figures. The economic cost of fish and wildlife mitigation can be estimated, within limits. Yet, the benefits of fish and wildlife mitigation are hard to evaluate, like other environmental benefits. Whether mitigation measures are successful may not be known for many years—perhaps not for several generations of a fish or wildlife species. Meanwhile, even though the economic constraint in the council's fish and wildlife program is weak legally, comparisons between quantifiable economic costs and unquantifiable biological benefits can be troubling. This puts a premium on finding measures of biological success, as evidence that this money is well spent.

Difficulty in predicting biological success is also a source of anxiety for fish and wildlife interests. Species may advance or decline from one year to another because of innumerable variables—power system operations, ocean conditions, water and climate conditions, and other powerful influences. In a year of decline, where there might be little concern in an entirely natural system, there is no way to know whether mitigation measures are failing, whether new or unforeseen problems are occurring, or whether natural variability is causing fluctuations that are beyond human control. Because fish and wildlife populations are so depressed, the temptation is to act, even though the problem may be unclear. As law professor Michael Blumm put it, this approach to fish and wildlife mitigation is "more uncertain, and it requires a kind of institutional sophistication that people who think as 'doers' have difficulty with, because they can't just do it." Acting in the face of uncertainty has risks.

The problem is reflected in the premise of adaptive management: biological success is hard even to measure, much less predict. For example, using the roughest measure of biological success—the aggregate salmon count—the current prospect is favorable. However, the picture for specific stocks is mixed. Some stocks once on the verge of extinction are now growing, while others are still in trouble. The region may yet face the possibility that the weakest salmon stocks may continue to decline despite mitigation efforts. An adaptive approach to mitigation implies that the results of these efforts will be surprising—encouraging and disappointing in turn. Gains expected may not materialize; efforts thought risky may turn out to be productive. Some populations may rise while others fall. As these new questions come up, the flexibility of the mitigation program and the adaptability of the power system—increasingly pressed to meet growing demand—will continue to be tested.

If biological measurement is likely to remain more art than science, however, the social and political benefits are easier to see. The region's fish and power interests have so far avoided the collision that appeared imminent in the early 1980s. Indian tribes, which once pushed management of the Columbia River fisheries into the federal courts, are major players in the council's program. Coalitions of government, tribal, and utility biologists have concentrated on designing and implementing the council's mitigation program. Experiments are being designed to probe key uncertainties, and monitoring and evaluation experts are working together to develop means for determining success or failure. The process is demanding—like changing a tire on an automobile that's going sixty miles an hour—and will grow more so. The prognosis is for a power system pushing for more speed and, the hope is, greater ability to fix flats and respond to environmental road signs.

SOME LESSONS FOR SUSTAINABLE WESTERN DEVELOPMENT

The Northwest offers a test case of what can emerge from collisions between economic development and environmental limitations. Apart from the obvious lesson that collisions are best avoided, what lessons can be learned from the Northwest's experience?

First, sustainable development requires a strategic view of development options and environmental resources. Gaining such a view requires an organization that is able to build on the diversity of existing institutions, and to harmonize this diversity. The Northwest example suggests that a state-based entity can take on this role if it has sufficient tools, including: (1) the commitment of federal agencies to implement the organization's strategic decisions; (2) a commitment that these strategic decisions will guide the investment of a significant pool of revenues, such as federal hydropower revenues; and (3) a process that includes widespread public participation.

Second, such organizations can find frameworks like least-cost planning that allow government and interested parties to understand how choices are connected to consequences—if a dam is built, for example, we may postpone a coal plant, but are there better energy conservation measures available that should be developed first? By stacking up and comparing a full range of development options, western government can develop better yardsticks with which to make these economic and environmental choices.

The third lesson is a corollary of the second. Conservation and efficiency measures must be looked at seriously in any broad examination of development options because conservation and efficiency are likely to be more cost-effective and less environmentally threatening than other kinds of development. Western communities are likely to turn first to conservation when economic and environmental conflicts become heated, as occurred in the Northwest. To avoid bringing such conflicts to a boil, developers must learn to build conservation and efficient resource use into development plans, and government must learn to look to conservation and efficiency measures as viable resources against which proposals for other development should be compared. Both developers and government agencies must become ingenious in finding ways to exploit conservation and other efficiencies.

The fourth lesson is that resource policy must be much more sensitive to uncertainty in economic and environmental decisions, and must develop techniques for managing risk. Uncertainty should not be allowed to paralyze decisions if steps can be taken to manage risk. One of the unexpected advantages of resource conservation and efficiency measures is their usefulness in managing uncertainty.

The fifth lesson is that sustainable development requires government to be pulled in two directions—environmental enhancement and economic development—rather than in one direction at the expense of the other. Conservation and resource efficiency may go a long way to stretch resources, but in many parts of the West the cumulative impacts of development have already run up against the West's physical, political, fiscal and legal carrying capacities. A commitment to environmental repair, protection, and enhancement is required to help expand these carrying capacities. The Northwest's experience permits few illusions about the difficulty of environmental recovery efforts. Environmental recovery is a costly enterprise in which short-term success is elusive. A long-term effort requires considerable patience in what can be a supercharged atmosphere.

The Northwest's approach does not exhaust the possibilities that are open to western states. Arrangements are likely to grow out of the unique circumstances of individual communities. Yet economic and environmental issues cannot effectively be addressed in fragments. With this in mind, the West must find ways to integrate environmental and development policy. The Northwest provides evidence that the West's diverse interests must, and can be, drawn into the process.

Sustainable development requires us to understand that economic needs and environmental consequences cannot be addressed separately, and finding ways to address them together is now an urgent task. While it took a crisis in the Northwest to develop mechanisms to deal with our water, power, and fisheries problems, we should look at these issues in a proactive way before positions become too entrenched. At the broadest level, the lesson taught by the Northwest's experience is that we must learn to make much more efficient use of resources in development, and to pay much more attention to replenishing environmental capital.

Government may play an important role in finding practical approaches to sustainable development in the West. Through policies that unify or fragment agency processes, account for or ignore environmental values, and recognize or mask uncertainties, government helps tip the balance for or against sustainable development. Sustainable natural resource policy may help western communities to develop with a view toward the long term, with confidence that their neighbors will follow suit.

The pressures that prompt the sustainable development debate do not necessarily threaten the West's prosperity. The Japanese, who have reduced the need for energy and materials in their domestic output by some 40 percent in ten years, and have done so while growing faster than any other major industrial country, have demonstrated one part of

Highway between Browning and East Glacier, Montana. Photo © George Wuerthner.

the lesson. Conservation and resource efficiency can create a competitive advantage. The West must learn to swim in the same waters, and yet do better than Japan, which has not escaped environmental problems of its own. The West must learn not just to be efficient, but also to understand its hole cards, and play its hand accordingly.

Pipeline, Alaska Range south of Delta junction. Photo © George Wuerthner.

Garrison Dam, North Dakota. Photo © Sheldon Green.

Hawaiian Highway. Photo © Jerry Chong.

By horseback and truck. Arizona. Photo © Monty Roessel.

Big Drops, Cataract Canyon, Colorado River above Lake Powell, Utah. Photo © John Telford.

Purse seiner. Valdez Arm, Prince William Sound, Alaska. Photo © George Wuerthner.

Herding sheep. Arizona. Photo © Monty Roessel.

Swathing. Red River Valley, North Dakota. Photo © Sheldon Green.

130

Cattle roundup in the Nebraska sandhills. Photo © Jon Farrar.

Aquaculture Farm, Oahu, Hawaii. Photo © Hugo deVries.

DOORS TO OUR HOUSE
William Kittredge

Dick Hugo used to say certain writers own certain words. The rest of us cannot use those words. Dick was thinking about Gerard Manley Hopkins and *dappled*. Should we use that lovely word, everybody would immediately think, Aha, derivative of Hopkins. It's true.

So, do not write anything about the dappled apples under the light in trees which bears apples. Not even if those apples lie around in the homestead of your memory. No matter what you do, the word *dappled* will ring of Gerard Manley Hopkins.

In the northern West certain writers have built for us a texture of metaphor around *sky—The Big Sky, Wind from an Enemy Sky, This House of Sky*—so it might be said they have found for us a way to claim emotional ownership of the word, and of its implications in our part of the world. Titles are names for whatever books are about, and among other things these books are about infinity and shelter, prospect and refuge, individualism and community. In them, like a set of mirrors, we have come to see ourselves and some of the psychic responsibilities inherent in inhabiting our piece of the earth from a perspective which is useful.

The jolt of recognition so many of us experienced when we first read *The Big Sky* had much to do with that title, and with what the book told us about the difficulties of staying humane when confronted with enormities of actual distances which often look to be unmappable. In the northern West we are always in danger of submitting to the implica-

Newspaper Rock State Park, Utah. Photo © Tom Till.

tions of those distances, and allowing ourselves the ruinous privilege of believing they are real and inevitable morally as well as physically. We are always tempted to find the difficulties of maintaining community too burdensome, and translating our physical isolations into indifference to the fate of others.

Think of Meriwether Lewis, as he came to the top of Lemhi Pass, imagining he would see some great highway of river toward the Pacific, instead confronted with ranges of mountains feathering off to a dim horizon with that terrifying expanse of sky beyond. It would be easy to see our own frailties written equally large when contemplating such real disconnections, and excuse ourselves anything. We might be tempted toward huddling into our fearfulness, cultivating the arts of selfishness. *The Big Sky* is among other things a cautionary tale telling us this temptation is no answer.

In *Wind from an Enemy Sky* D'Arcy McNickle showed us the far and even darker side of the same predicament, native communities shattered by the unfathomable imperialistic gusts of what is called civilization. When Ivan Doig entitled his book *This House of Sky* he was taking on big medicine, reaffirming and at the same time amending notions about the importance of that shelter which is family, and of the ultimately coherent self which grows out of family.

These are powerful books, and the central metaphor which helps generate their power—*sky*—is located securely in place, in region, in Montana and the northern West. Through the act of finding such a metaphor, and exploring it, these writers made it a gift to those of us who live here. We look out to our distances through the lens of that notion in its complexities, and we see meaning. Through generations of living in this difficult place, with the help of our artists, we have come to possess resonances that help fill our silences. This kind of emotional ownership is as close as we will ever come, really, to owning any place.

The way I see it now is that you either make a little nation and solve its historical and personal problems within the format of your own household—accepting the mistakes that you've made, all the ones your parents made, and all that your children make, and all the mistakes your country has made—and you win that one or you lose the only war worth fighting.

Moreover, as soon as you step out of this personally constructed world and, say, drive into town or stand out on I-90 and watch our nation cycle through these placeless arteries, it's there that you confront the true horror of the other option.

Thomas McGuane, interviewed in *The Paris Review*

A few years ago *The New York Times Book Review* sent David Quammen around to interview people and write a piece about ''Montana Writers.'' In Missoula, some people got together in the Eastgate Liquor Lounge, as they did in those days, and Quammen quizzed us about why so many writers have settled in Montana. Max Crawford, a Texan who was living in town at the time, said it was because writers needed to live cheap.

''It's like Paris in the 1920s,'' Max said. ''All those writers talked like it was Paradise, but soon as the exchange rate dropped they all went home.''

While never doubting that money is real important, since it can equal freedom for an artist, I tend to believe that writers and other artists are congregating in Montana and its environs for reasons beyond money— like the possibility of living in the local company of peers, connected to a place knowable in human terms, where you can walk around like a citizen in a recognizable community.

But I can also understand where Max Crawford was coming from. Max was outraged by the idea of being tagged a regional, and therefore a minor writer. This is where I have trouble. I don't see the conjunction of 'regional' and 'minor'.

What I mean to argue, in fact, is that art has a much greater chance if it starts in a particular place, like Oxford in Mississippi, and moves out toward the Nobel Prize. Think of it this way: we all have our complaints about television and movies, the imperial art of our culture. The run of it is superficial and silly. We wonder if it has to be that way, and if so, why?

The answer seems simple enough. Driven by enormous production and distribution expenses, movies and television must draw huge coast-to-coast audiences if they are to pay their bills. So they tell stories about some homogenized America which does not exist except in dream, a never-never land. It's art designed for the widest possible audience, all of America and the world overseas and as such it isn't about anybody, really, and it's not centered anywhere actual. How could it speak to any of us in our deepest, most local concerns? There are exceptions, of course, since most good film and TV people are deeply aware of these concerns. But the complaint continues to be valid: our most pervasive art forms are our most superficial.

At the recent Montana History Conference in Helena some people from Fort Peck exhibited and talked about the Star Quilts made by women on the Reservation, and people from the college in Pablo on the Flathead Reservation showed us a video tape of a women doing fine work with deer and elk hides. Those people showed us arts which had evolved in a local place, in response to complex abilities and needs, over generations. The art reflected particular people as they responded to the actualities of their lives and histories, and because of that it was unique and singular—speaking to us of individual relationships to beauty and attempts to define what is sacred. We are moved by such art, when we are moved, because in it we see ourselves striving to make sense of things, continually redefining our notions of what is valuable. Such identification encourages us to be humane.

What I'm trying to say is that regional art is important because it is mostly the only art which is useful in our efforts to know ourselves, even if only locally. And there are times when it transcends its regionality. No art could be more securely located in a particular time and place than *The Iliad* or *Don Quixote* or *Moby Dick* or Shakespeare or Sophocles or *The Canterbury Tales* or *Remembrance of Things Past*. Or the great wood carving done by Tsimshian and Haida and Tlingit artists along the Northwest Coast of North America. Make your own list: most of the great stuff starts local, rooted in one-of-a-kind lives and communities, maybe Plentywood or some house on a side street in Paris.

I have never distinguished readily between thinking and dreaming. I know my life would be much different if I could ever say, This I have learned from my senses, while that I have merely imagined. I will try to tell you the plain truth.

Marilynne Robinson, *Housekeeping*

Over the last fifty or sixty years artists in the American West have gone through a long and difficult battle, claiming and reclaiming their emotional homeland. It's fair to say that up until the 1930s most major art set in the American West was centered around the myth of The Western: gunslingers and settlers and savages, invading armies and law-bringing.

Not that the myth didn't spring from some actual anecdotes. It's just that our out-West experiences were taken over by storytellers eager to satisfy audiences more interested in romance than in any real story. Even an artist like Charlie Russell, so deeply rooted in the gone-hungry dustiness of daily life in Montana, so concerned about getting each detail right, did not escape.

Russell's paintings for the most part portray the great romance of the Western—strong heedless figures on an enormous, gorgeous landscape. Charlie Russell came West to find adventure, and he painted the adventure he found. It's easy to understand why his work remains so popular in the hometown he found and loved, Great Falls, and all over the West. His paintings tell us our lives are connected to great doings in a grand sweep of mythological story, and significant. Russell saw through the lens of that story, and painted what it allowed him to see.

Mark Twain looked to the East, from where the culture came, wrote the silliness of *Roughing It* for an eastern audience, and then migrated as quickly as he could to New York to celebrate his literary triumph. Buffalo Bill's Wild West Show performed before sell-out crowds in Europe, but surely told little of truth or importance. And even early on, some were nettled by the bald nonsense. In Wild Bill Hickock's first stage venture the script called for him to sit by a crepe paper campfire, sipping whiskey and spinning yarns. On opening night Hickock took a healthy

Regional art is important because it is mostly the only art which is useful in our efforts to know ourselves . . .

139

swig of what proved to be cold tea, spat it onto the boards, and bellowed, "I ain't telling no lies until I get some real whiskey."

The myth has been an insidious trap for those who would write about the American West, a box for the imagination. For a long time it was as if there was only one legitimate story to tell about the West, and that was the mythological story.

William Eastlake once told me to never let a publisher put a picture of a horse on the cover of any novel I might publish. "The people who buy it will think it's some goddamned shoot up," Eastlake said. "And they'll hate it when it isn't."

Eastlake was saying that western writers somehow have to insist that the real, emotionally possessed life they grew up inside of, or found when they came to the country—as opposed to the stylized morality play that was supposed to be western experience—was worth writing about. Many of us have shared the difficulty of working when expected to write from inside myth. But it's not so bad anymore, mostly because of the hard labor of some widely disparate writers we can think of as drawing together under an ungainly label: *antimythological.*

In 1903 Andy Adams published *Log of a Cowboy,* detailing a late nineteenth-century cattle drive from northern Mexico to the Blackfeet reservation in northern Montana. The story is reasonably accurate and well told. Talking of days in the saddle and without drinking water, of dust and cold wind and putting your saddle in a gunnysack at drive's end and taking the train home to Texas. It was a life with no room for the lacy-sleeved mythological six-gun exhibitions of Main Street gamblers.

Willa Cather was born in 1873, grew up in Red Lodge, Nebraska, met Stephen Crane, determined herself on a career in writing, moved to work as an editor in New York for a while, became a lover of women, and eventually took the advice of Sarah Orne Jewett to "find your own quiet center of life and write from that."

It's an old story with American artists. Having gone into exile in New York or Paris or some far-away land which may exist only in the mind, they find imaginative freedom to look home. Think of Hemingway looking back to Michigan, or Max Crawford in Missoula during the early

1980s, writing his fine, under-valued novel about the history of his home country in west Texas, *Lords of the Plain.* In 1918 Cather published her famous novel of Nebraska life, *My Antonia.*

Ole Rölvaag was born in Norway, in 1876. At the age of twenty he emigrated to his uncle's farm in South Dakota, went off to school, and at thirty became a teacher at St. Olaf College. At the age of fifty, in 1926, he published his great gone-crazy-in-the-distances story of Norwegian emigrant life on the Dakota plains, *Giants in the Earth.*

By the 1930s, off obscure in the Sand Hills of Nebraska, a girl named Mari Sandoz, likely inspired by the example of Willa Cather and Rölvaag, had matured tough enough on a homestead ranch. She was making ready to write a book about her father—who was one of those damned old litigious autodidact unbathed loons we find all over the West—and the women who kept him functioning. At the end of her story she tells of Jules in his death bed, finding a newspaper item about a writing contest she had won. As she tells it: "He tore the paper across, ordered a pencil and paper brought, wrote her one line in the old, firm, up-and-down strokes: 'You know I consider artists and writers the maggots of society.' "

Why wouldn't he? Hadn't they told nothing but lies about the strenuous facts of life where he had lived, the turn of endless horizon and the turkey-packed earth where the wash-water was flung outside the back door of the ranch house, season after season as the generations passed? Mari Sandoz gives this eulogy:

> Outside the late fall wind swept over the hard-land country of the upper Running Water, tearing at the low sandy knolls that were the knees of the hills, shifting, but not changing, the unalterable sameness of the somnolent land spreading away to the east.

Jules could not know that Mari, like H. L. Davis, John Steinbeck, Walter van Tilburg Clark, Wallace Stegner, A. B. Guthrie, Jr., and an assortment of others less well known, was getting ready to write books which would attempt to convey the emotional truth of the various western lives they had lived and witnessed and come to possess while inhabiting the country. Jules died in 1928.

Old Jules was published in 1935. It ought to be one of the sacred white-man texts for writers in the modern West. If you start reading around in journals and diaries and letters from the early West, mostly written by women, you will find a quite different story than those written for publication in the East. For instance, you will hardly ever find a holy gunslinger come from the wilderness to right the troubles of society. Instead you will find—how to put it?—the perfect eccentricities of everyday life, your local and quite detailed Weather Reports, both sacred and demonic, mental and otherwise. You will find the so-called 'real' life as she was experienced, snakes, dust, sod-house walls, wash-water and all. And you will find the same sort of item in *Old Jules*: the splintery texture of the actual, sanded a little by art, but there like rocks beneath the water.

Willa Cather and Ole Rölvaag and Mari Sandoz got away to school and learned some craft, and then went home to write up the verities they had learned nearby, while they were at it finding for us in the American West a set of beginnings: what we might think of as a literature springing from experience, not much like the romantic and nonsensical, melodramatic morality play which is The Western.

The doors were open; the idea was in the air; and the good books came, each helping free us to the notion that the specific instances of our lives might be a fit subject, if somebody could manage it, for that *old Beau Ideal,* high art. Out in Oregon, in 1935, H. L. Davis won the Pulitzer Prize for *Honey In the Horn.* Walter van Tilburg Clark published *The Ox-Bow Incident* in 1940; Wallace Stegner published *The Big Rock Candy Mountain* in 1943; Bud Guthrie published *The Big Sky* in 1947. All this chronology is maybe just the hindsight detailing of what we want to see, but by one means or another the next generations of western writers have taken heart from it.

Listen to Wallace Stegner, from *The Big Rock Candy Mountain*:

Things greened up beautifully that June. Rains came up out of the southeast, piling up solidly, moving toward them as slowly and surely as the sun moved, and it was fun to watch them come, the three of them standing in the doorway. When they saw the land to the east of them darken under the rain Bo would say, "Well, doesn't look as if it's going to miss us," and they would jump to shut the windows and bring things in from the yard or clothesline. Then they could stand quietly in the door and watch the rain come, the front of it like a wall and the wind ahead of it stirring up dust, until it reached them and drenched the bare packed earth of the yard, and the ground smoked under its feet, and darkened, and rain in little streams, and they heard the swish of rain on roof and ground and in the air.

And this, from the story "Carrion Spring," in *Wolf Willow:*

Three days of chinook had uncovered everything that had been under the snow since November. The yard lay discolored and ugly, gray ash pile, rusted cans, spilled lignite, bones. The clinkers that had given them winter footing for the privy and stable lay in raised gray wafers across the mud; the strung lariats they had used for lifelines in the blizzard weather had dried out and sagged to the ground. Mud was knee-deep down in the corrals by the sod-roofed stable, the white-washed logs were yellowed at the corners from dogs lifting their legs against them. Sunken drifts around the hay yard were a reminder of how many times the boys had had to shovel out there to keep the calves from walking into the stacks across the top of the snow. Across the wan and disheveled yard the willows were bare, and beyond them the floodplain hill was brown. The sky was roiled with gray cloud.

A generation of writers were proving that the West had more compelling stores than those of simpleminded gunplay, that the private lives lived in the West were worth writing about just as any life is worth art if, in seeing it through the eyes of the artist, we are helped to see our own life with renewed clarity.

And they never thought they'd have a girl from this reservation as a saint they'd have to kneel to. But they'd have me. And I'd be carved in pure gold. With ruby lips. And my toenails would be little

A generation of writers were proving that the West had more compelling stories than those of simpleminded gunplay . . .

143

pink ocean shells, which they would have to stoop down off their high horses to kiss.

Louise Erdrich, *Love Medicine*

Try this for openers: the art of a region begins to come mature when it is no longer what we think it should be.

Imagine 1929, reading *The Sound and the Fury* in the deep South. How crazy that book must have seemed, how unsettling and unreal, actual. But, if you want a sweeping, over-simplified but part-ways true generalization, grown-up Southern literature began there. Right away Faulkner was followed by Eudora Welty, Robert Penn Warren, Katherine Anne Porter, Carson McCullers, and Flannery O'Connor.

Clearly, even without a genius like Faulkner to get things started, the same sort of phenomenon is taking place all over the inland reaches of the American West. Back in the middle '70s Dorothy Johnson sent me a book to review for the local newspaper. "I don't know if this is any good," she said. "It's sure got a strange title." She went on to tell me the author was a man who had grown up in Missoula, then gone off to spend his life teaching at the University of Chicago. The book, of course, was *A River Runs Through It.*

And indeed, it seemed pretty strange to me. *In our family there was no clear line between religion and fly fishing.* Now was that any way to start a story in the West? About halfway through the news began to sink in.

This was not just some odd set of memories written down by an old man. This was the real goddamned thing, Literature, and the climatic events took place alongside a fishing hole where I had been skunked only the week before. In retrospect, that was when I first began to suspect the West was going to have itself an adult literature. I mean, there had been some terrific books in recent years, *House Made of Dawn, Desert Solitaire, The Milagro Beanfield War, Ceremony, Winter in the Blood,* Dick Hugo—but for me it was Maclean, so quirky and rock-solid and unexpected, who pointed out that the doors of possibility were open wide.

Sometimes it is a comfort to believe that one day is like another, that things happen over and over and are the same. But accidents happen, and sometimes a man or a woman is lucky enough to see that all of it, from the first light kiss onward, could have gone another way.

David Long, *Home Fires*

So, out in our West, artists are trying to run their eyes clear of mythic and legendary cobwebs, and see straight to the actual. But sometimes you have to wonder about that. As a friend of mine says, "I ask for truth, and what do I get? Candor."

You have to suspect that much of the attraction of Evan Connell's best-selling Custer book, *Son of Morning Star,* comes from its willingness to tell anything, the sense it conveys that this is the real story with blinders off. It's a book that reeks of atrocious detail, atrocity after atrocity. You have to stay a little leery of such impulses. Maybe it's truth, and maybe it's only a chronicle of sensational murdering, no more meaningful than the front page of the local paper, with its daily bloodbaths.

Or not. You also have to be edgy about such categorizing. You run into books like *Blood Meridian* by Cormac MacCarthy, a recent novel about scalp-hunting in the Southwest after the Mexican War, a story so beautiful and vivid with horror it makes your worst dreams look like popcorn, and you don't know what to say.

Let it go at this: there is indeed a new candor afoot in the land. Maybe it's part of the impulse to see straight to the beating meaningful heart of things, but sometimes it's only hearts torn apart while we watch: candor, a manifestation of our nostalgia for the old days when violence seemed meaningful.

Anyway, it probably all helps clear the decks. For what? Quickly now, we will stagger through a list of my favorites, writers who are coming to maturity in the West, or writing about the West in mature ways, most of them not exactly famous yet: Bill Yellow Robe, Robert Wrigley, Roberta Hill Whiteman, David Long, Douglas Unger, Richard Ford, Sandra Alcosser, David Quammen, Gretel Ehrlich, Patricia Henley,

Ralph Beer, Paul Zarzyski, Mary Blew, Marilynne Robinson, Louise Erdrich, Jim Welch, Edward Abbey, Leslie Marmon Silko, Cyra McFadden, Tom McGuane, Elizabeth Tallent, Ivan Doig, John Keeble.

I'm out of breath, and out of faith with this kind of listing. It seemed a good idea while I had the chance, but it doesn't mean much. I apologize to those left off because of my ignorance. Read the work, and find your own favorites.

The point is, they come from all over the place, Montana City, Santa Barbara, upstate Wisconsin, the Mississippi Delta, New York City, and live all over the place, few of them much over forty, and they are doing work strange and varied as the country. What if we listen to a few lines from *Love Medicine* by Louise Erdrich, and *Housekeeping* by Marilynne Robinson, novels private and immaculate as the inside of a cat's mouth, and then shut up and think things over? Like this, from *Love Medicine,* set on a reservation in North Dakota:

> Your life feels different on you, once you greet death and understand your heart's position. You wear your life like a garment from the mission bundle sale ever after—lightly because you realize you never paid anything for it, cherishing because you know you won't come by such a bargain again. Also you have the feeling someone wore it before you and someone will after.

And this, from *Housekeeping,* set over in Sand Point, Idaho:

> Of my conception I know only what you know of yours. It occurred in darkness and I was unconsenting. I (and that slenderest word is too gross for what I was then) walked forever through reachless oblivion, in the mood of one smelling night-blooming flowers, and suddenly—My ravishers left their traces in me, male and female, and over months I rounded, grew heavy, until the scandal could no longer be concealed and oblivion expelled me. But this I have in common with all my kind. By some bleak alchemy what had been mere unbeing becomes death when life is mingled with it. So they seal the door against our returning.

Essay excerpted from *Owning It All*, published by Graywolf Press. Reprinted with permission.

Grant Kohrs Ranch National Historic Site, Deer Lodge, Montana. Photo © George Wuerthner.

North of Santa Fe, Sangre de Cristo Mountains, New Mexico. Photo © George Wuerthner.

Downtown Anchorage, Alaska. Photo © George Wuerthner.

View from Camels Back Park, Boise, Idaho. Photo © Brent Smith.

Arco, Idaho. Photo © Brent Smith.

Pacific Coast Highway,
California. Photo ©
Los Angeles Visitors
and Convention
Bureau.

Container shipping,
Honolulu, Hawaii.
Photo © Hugo deVries.

Minot, North Dakota.
Photo © Sheldon
Green.

152

Mountain America Building, Salt Lake City, Utah. Photo © John Telford.

Wendover, Nevada. Photo © George Wuerthner.

Wupatki National Monument, Arizona. Photo © Tom Till.

Pueblo Bonito, Chaco Culture National Historic Site, New Mexico. Photo © Tom Till.

Abandoned homestead, Grand Teton National Park, Wyoming. Photo © George Wuerthner.

Rock Springs, Wyoming. Photo © John Telford.

THE PHOTOGRAPHERS

Jerry Chong
Turner & deVries
1200 College Walk, Suite 212
Honolulu, Hawaii 96817

Hugo deVries
Turner & deVries
1200 College Walk, Suite 212
Honolulu, Hawaii 96817

Jon Farrar
Box 4436
Lincoln, Nebraska 68504

Sheldon Green
P.O. Box 2497
Fargo, North Dakota 58108

Kent Knudsen
6219 N. 9th Place
Phoenix, Arizona 85014

Steven Meckler
6219 N. 9th Place
Phoenix, Arizona 85014

Martin Price
708 Arapahoe Avenue
Boulder, Colorado 80302

Monty Roessel
P.O. Box 0034
Roundrock Tours, Arizona 86547

Brent Smith
3202 N. Mountain Lane
Boise, Idaho 83702

John Telford
1571 Casper Rd.
Salt Lake City, Utah 84092

Tom Till
P.O. Box 337
Moab, Utah 84532

George Wuerthner
P.O. Box 273
Livingston, Montana 59047

THE AUTHORS

STEWART L. UDALL was born in St. Johns, Arizona. He was a three-term congressman from Arizona and went on to serve as Secretary of the Interior for eight years during the Kennedy and Johnson administrations. He is the author of *The Quiet Crisis* and *To the Inland Empire.* He currently resides in Santa Fe, New Mexico.

PATRICIA NELSON LIMERICK was born in Banning, California. She received her undergraduate degree from the University of California at Santa Cruz and her Ph.D. in American Studies from Yale. She taught at Yale and Harvard before moving to the University of Colorado in 1984, where she is currently Associate Professor of History specializing in history of the American West. She is the author of *Desert Passages* and *The Legacy of Conquest: The Unbroken Past of the American West.*

CHARLES F. WILKINSON, currently the Moses Lasky Professor of Law at the University of Colorado, is one of the nation's leading scholars and lecturers on issues relating to natural resources law and policy in the American West. He is the author of two standard law texts, and his most recent books are *The American West—A Critical Bibliography and a Study in Regionalism* and *The Eagle Bird—Searching for an Ethic of Place.*

JOHN M. VOLKMAN was raised in Salt Lake City, Utah, and Fresno, California. He graduated from the Colorado College and the University of Colorado Law School, and in 1973 moved to Portland, Oregon. Since 1985 he has represented the Northwest Power Planning Council (his views in this essay do not necessarily reflect those of the council), where he handles natural resource law issues involving the four Northwest states. He has dedicated his chapter to his wife, Stephanie, and his children, Jessie and Caitlin.

WILLIAM KITTREDGE grew up on the MC Ranch in southeastern Oregon, farmed until he was thirty-five, studied in the Writer's Workshop at the University of Iowa, and is presently a Professor of English and Creative Writing at the University of Montana. He coedited *The Last Best Place: A Montana Anthology,* and his most recent books are a collection of short fiction, *We Are Not In This Together,* and a collection of essays *Owning It All.*